Money uck

Money uck

How greed & unfair practices created an unbearable society

Jim McCurdy

iUniverse, Inc.
New York   Bloomington

Money uck
How greed & unfair practices created an unbearable society

Copyright © 2010 by Jim McCurdy

iUniverse books may be ordered through booksellers or by contacting:

iUniverse
1663 Liberty Drive
Bloomington, IN 47403
www.iuniverse.com
1-800-Authors (1-800-288-4677)

ISBN: 978-1-4502-6154-8 (sc)
ISBN: 978-1-4502-6155-5 (ebk)

Printed in the United States of America

iUniverse rev. date: 11/01/2010

"It's evil and it's not good and everyone should just burn it."
— Bernd Friedlander, a San Francisco area doctor

"Money changes certain people. In general, people just want to make enough money to survive. The rich people get a lot of breaks. You've got a few greedy, powerful people who control everything."
— a former Chicago Bulls insider who shared a close friendship with a financial genius who studied the currency system from the floors of the New York stock market

"Teaching from your lips is more precious to me than heaps of silver and gold."
— Psalm 119:72
"A Prayer to God, the Lawgiver"
(The New American Bible)

"No one can serve two masters. He will either hate one and love the other, or be devoted to one and despise the other. You cannot serve God and mammon."
— **Jesus**
(as quoted in Matthew 6:24)

Table of Contents

Chapter 1
Rethinking resources   7

Chapter 2
Education, edification & ethics ... eerie   35

Chapter 3
Buying into banking   46

Chapter 4
Bashing business   72

Chapter 5
Pocket-poking stories   113

Chapter 6
Fixing finances   127

S ome might argue we must first define what money is before we start breaking down its baggage.

What is it to you? What is it to the next person? What is it to those who make the money?

Whatever definition you have for money — something that people continuously think about nowadays, isn't really the issue. The issue is the type of buying power money has and how it affects the way we are able to live nowadays. How much leverage does it give you? What can you use it for? Do you really need any of it to get by in life and make you happy? Are you struggling to survive because you don't have enough of it?

These days, most people will go to whatever means they feel necessary to obtain money. Including stealing.

What happened to sticking to the Bible passages in which Jesus told people you cannot follow God and money? Money in the Bible is also referred to as mammon.

Consider it documented. Translated. Detailed. Passed on. Slightly altered. Revised. However you want to look at it, why the wording in one Bible version may slightly differ from the next, the bottom line is clear.

When you chase money, you're not chasing God.

Money uck.

Is money truly the root of all evil? Some may wish to debate that, but most people probably wouldn't argue. Scripture doesn't lie, either. Surely, the love of money is the root of evil.

Today's way of thinking has become all about looking out for No. 1. Call it controlling your own capitalism. Call it greed. We've all heard this notion of "the rich get richer and the poor get poorer." Whatever phrase you want to coin about this current currency system is your choice.

Bottom line, money sucks.

Money has caused so many problems in society that even the idea of it has turned people against each other in many ways. It's ruined marriages, relationships and friendships.

"Prenuptial agreements ... built-in disaster," a preacher delivered in a Sunday sermon in September 2007.

Money has forced people to be judged by a score attached to the rear end of their name. It's caused friction amongst loving people for, when it really boils down to it, no apparent reason.

Dollars have made starving people suffer more. And why?

Because some people have it, and others don't. Some people aren't willing to spread their wealth, and others simply don't have enough to share. For those who have a surplus of money, that can mean only one thing.

Greed.

The idea of acquiring more money has caused the universe's richest people to obtain the majority of the shrinking dollar, forcing others to lose more of it. In turn, those losing out on the green are fighting for escapes. Searching for answers. Waiting for someone to help in a world that seems to keep saying, "No."

Want milk?

Give us money.

Give us more, we'll be happy and you'll be on good terms. Give us less and we don't like you. Can't deal with you. Can't help you. Sorry.

That's one way of looking at it.

Guess what? It's wrong. And people better start changing their ways soon or there are going to be severe consequences. Consequences that are beyond a human being's control. Only divine intervention can step in then, and that's what it may come down to.

Do not be fooled, this idea about turning total attention toward money is real. It is running rampant nowadays, and it has influenced people to do things many people have never even thought of, let alone simply won't accept. It's resulted in responses that people simply don't want to hear. It's caused people to kill other people. It's shredded apart those numbers attached to the end of your last name.

Sorry, don't have the money? Can't pay for it? Bend over because your credit score is about to slap you in the butt.

Money has caused people to fret about the dangers and perils of the unknown. "If I don't get enough now, I don't know what I'll do," people say. Money is so complex, only the money makers themselves don't have a true handle on it. The money makers don't understand the concept completely enough to help those who need it most. Or they simply don't want to help those in need. If they really cared about other human beings they would make more of it, disperse it in equal parts or change the system. But those in control aren't doing enough to help those who don't have enough money. In turn, the world is becoming filled with more stress, anxiety and unruly actions.

Why can't there be a more equitable system?

Ask the money makers. Ask leaders responsible for looking out for everyone's best interest. That is, if you can get to them. That is, if they give you the time of day. That is, if they have the courage to let the rest in on their secrets. In order to get them to talk, you'll probably need money. Not even the freedoms set up many moons ago seem to be freedoms anymore.

Oh how Benjamin Franklin and Thomas Jefferson are pulling grey hairs out now.

Banks are greedy. Corporations. Big business. Universities, colleges. Professional sports. The entertainment industry. They're all in search of the almighty dollar. Let's not forget, there are an awful lot of greedy individuals courting cash, too. Were you aware that until 2007 when greed began to catch up to itself in the form of a major recession, Atlantic City casinos had brought in more money every year since the East Coast gaming industry opened?

Donald Trump, do elaborate.

Everyone seems to be operating with the sole purpose of coveting money. Forget about the idea of providing a service to actually help someone. It's all about how much you have in order to secure that service. And the stakes keep growing. The same way inflation never ceases.

Speaking of which, what really does inflation accomplish anyway? Backlash, more debt, more problems, more fighting, more struggles. The shrinking dollar and rising costs lend itself to only one logical solution.

No logic.

Knock, knock. Hello, brain trusts. Are you there? People are starving, you're raising costs, telling people to buy homes, and building supplies and labor keep going up. But wages aren't changing.

Hello.

Educators, what really is in your best interest? Teaching toddlers and mature students or fattening your wallets? And what for in the long run, really? To give people an educational base to … make money.

Money to eat. Money to pay rapidly-rising bills. Money to live in an increasingly suffocating society.

Money to survive.

People soon begin to worry, "Once my money runs out, I'll be doomed. No money means no survival. Or at least it will be a whole lot tougher. So I just have to go get more of it now."

Problem is, there's only so much to go around.

Problem is, not everyone's going to get it under the current system.

Why?

It's that five-letter word again that starts with "g."

And it ain't great.

Chapter 1

Rethinking resources

"If there were no money ... the arms race, there would be peace."

— A Catholic priest
September 23, 2007

I t's awfully sad when you consider your future — the one determined by society's standards — that you might not have much of a future.

Before you put this book down and dismiss the rest, realize this: money, and the lack thereof, has affected people in agonizing, unfair and unethical ways. Until something is changed, problems will persist, people will die for unwarranted reasons. Others, innocent or not, will be hurt in grueling, unfair ways.

Money at the crux of the problem, of course.

On Jan. 23, 2007, *USA Today* ran a front page article, headlined, "Retirees Up Against DEBT."

The concept of retiring into debt is a scary, bone-chilling thought indeed. All these years, we've entrusted our currency system to a bunch of people at the top who can't even figure out a way to make retirement equitable. Or don't want to make retirement equitable.

People have to work to live. Even when they aren't even capable of working.

Sad.

The *USA Today* article reported the following:

Retirement used to be a time for people to enjoy life without a mortgage or high credit card bills, a time when heavy debts were mostly a thing of the past. Increasingly, that's no longer true. Some seniors are taking on debt in retirement to fund a trip they've always wanted to take. But a growing number are in debt because they have no choice, according to debt counselors and a growing body of research.

Soaring health care costs are hitting seniors at a time when more employers are cutting back on retiree medical and pension benefits. People are living longer. Yet many seniors subsist on fixed incomes, and have little means to boost their incomes.

From 1992 to 2004, the percentage of households 55 and older with overall debt grew faster than the rate of the overall population. Those 75 and older packed it on most quickly: The average load for those households with debt shot up 160% to an average of $20,234 during this time, according *to research by the Employee Benefit Research Institute, a non-partisan group that studies economic security.*

Among households 65 and older, the average amount of credit card debt more than doubled from 1992 to 2004, to $4,907, according to Demos, a New York think tank. Seniors' debt levels are catching up to younger people.

Seniors in and approaching retirement — such as the oldest baby boomers — are carrying "debt loads that their parents would not have considered," says Sally Hurme of AARP, the advocacy group for people 50 and older. "This does not bode well for financial wealth."

People have turned their thoughts nowadays toward money and greed. Knowingly or unknowingly.

It's because of the way the system is set up.

In January of 2007 at the Barrett-Jackson Collection Car Auction in Scottsdale, Ariz., a 1966 Shelby Cobra Super Snake sold for $5.5 million. It was reported as a world record at an auction. A car, for $5.5 million. C'mon.

Indeed, people are going after what's wrong in the world. Case in point, war in Iraq. At its crux, what did it all center on? Some argue it was all about terrorism. Others would disagree, insisting oil played a major role. And why? Money. Some argue if the United States had no oil this country would be done.

Some say controlling the oil will be a way to control the world.

Controlling the world nowadays has a lot to do with controlling money.

Did you know almost *all* of the money supply in the world is controlled by the slightest fraction of people. Something to the tune of 96 percent of the money supply is monopolized by roughly 1 percent of the population.

Horrifying.

Some in this life remain at the top and don't look down with much regard for the people underneath. Otherwise, they'd do more to help. Some have good intentions. Either way, there is no equilibrium.

The system isn't fair.

Multi-billionaires. Billionaires. Those are people who make money off of your money without really flinching too much. And too many people, those no where near billionaire status, think they can make people do what they want them to do because they have money. Until they run into the wrong person. One who's not caught up in money. One who doesn't just react when a millionaire, with apologies to Ludacris, shakes their money maker or waves their magic wand and says, "do this."

Guess what million dollar baby, some people just aren't going to react by your magic-moving words. They see the phony side in it all. These are the people who must put in a lot of sweat equity just to get the ball rolling to get the bills rolling. People who aren't moved by money.

Like the Bible says, those who humble themselves shall be exalted.

Around the turn of the new millennium, some reports claimed the U.S. dollar supply was around 6 trillion. Those same reports also stated that amount of money would only run the American federal government for a couple years. Whether those reports were pinpoint accurate, slightly incorrect or even so far off isn't the issue. After all, there are different methods used in counting what is considered real money. Real money, to some, is defined as cash or checking account funds. But who really dictates how much money people are going to get? Some argue it's all up to yourself. Some say even those with the most brilliant ideas can't cut it because others don't want to allow them the opportunity to do so.

What essentially determines how far your limitations take you boils down to those in control. The government, big bucks businesses, big banks or financial institutions and the CEOs or people in charge — they're major players who have the majority say in it all.

Donna Bullard, CEO of a Clarkston, Mich., credit union, was asked whether she'd ever accept gold as a deposit to open an account or as a form of payment. Bullard stumbled. She searched for an answer. Frankly, she didn't have an answer. It almost sounded if she feared her response would be audited.

"Regulators would, of course, be telling us what we could and could not do," Bullard said, a bit unsure of her answer. "We're all regulated by the state or federal or both. I really wouldn't know how to answer that."

Exactly, let the regulators figure it out because they've got all the answers.

Not to mention a lot of the money.

According to Turbo Tax, of all the tax returns filed in 2004, 28 percent fell into the $0- 14,999 adjusted gross income range. That's below poverty in many standards. That's over a quarter of all people who filed taxes. The national average for net loss was $-13,879.

The report also listed the following data:

National Average
Interest and Dividends
$7,996

Net Capital Gain
$7,046

Net Capital Loss
-$2,430

IRA Withdrawals
$4,634

Pensions and Annuities

$6,892

Social Security Benefits
$4,131

These numbers represent averages for tax filers. And they are figures that don't suggest much room for forgiveness for people short on funds.

What is money?

Some people consider money a means of trade, a means of getting something for what one is willing to give up. Barter. Trade. Exchange. That could mean time. It could mean paper currency. It could mean physical objects.

Aubie Baltin, a retired chartered financial analyst, commodity trading advisor and certified financial planner who held a doctoral degree from McGill University in Montreal, believes he knows what money truly is all about.

"Money is an inanimate object," Baltin said shortly after publishing a 2007 financial forecast in which he talked about the declining U.S. dollar.

Baltin defines money this way:

M1, money supply, consists of cash plus checking accounts and travelers checks. M2 consists of M1 plus retail money market funds, savings and small time deposits. M3 consists of M2 plus large-time deposits, Eurodollars & large money market funds.

M1, M2, M3, whatever. Money is simply problematic. And the reason why problems persist may seem perplexing, but they're not impossible to solve.

"This is a mistake that most people, including economists, make," Baltin said. "We're always trying to treat the effect. You can never find a cure if you're always chasing the effect. You can't fix it if you don't look for the problem."

So how do we fix the current currency constraints? We'll save specific details for later.

For now, you could start by finding more intelligent people to make better decisions on the way the economy is run and how the money supply is allocated. Oh, how Ross Perot is saying, "I told you so," now. You could produce more money and distribute it evenly to people in need. Hardworking, willing to work people, heck even those who can't find a place to live because of that ugly stereotype they're constantly haunted by. Many times the homeless can't secure jobs because they don't have money to shave or buy clothes — all factors in which they're judged by other humans.

Or you could just get rid of money altogether.

Why not? Especially considering it would be easier to just exchange a handshake and a favor to acquire something than it would be to try to work for 10 years just to have money to use as a down payment on house.

"Money is a meeting of exchange," Baltin insisted. "Money just facilitates a trade."

Nowadays, in a very unfair system.

Gold used to hold similar value. Kind of the way oil became a hot commodity. President Richard Nixon nixed the idea of placing too much weight in gold in 1971 when he dismembered it as a form of currency because people living outside the United States were laying claims to gold instead of dollars. The United States wanted it known that the country's almighty dollar was the most dominant force in currency.

Little did we know, America would become so extremely troubled by debt that the almighty dollar would create almighty problems. But we can thank those at the top for that.

"The government that governs least governs best," Baltin said.

That's what the forefathers of the United States, the 13 original colonies, believed. Their words in the Declaration of Independence haven't disappeared. But somewhere along the way their ideas have.

Died.

Vanished.

Evaporated.

Sadly, corporate minds became the norm.

If you've got money, you've got what you need. At least that's what some people think.

So the gold diggers, be it from their 49er days in San Francisco or chance inheritance, turned the tables. They started putting higher price tags on gold, hyping it up and subsequently started selling more gold on a retail level to cash in on the almighty dollar.

Heck, why not? The government didn't want to recognize gold as a means of exchange. So why not build up the hype over gold and start selling it? That way, people thought, they could profit and do what they saw fit with their earnings.

As it turned out, digging for gold wasn't such a bad idea. In 2006, a buzz circulated about gold resurfacing, becoming a viable means of exchange. Simultaneously, the U.S. dollar's image continued to take its share of tarnishing blows. And questions lingered why the country that produces the mighty dollar only has so much of it to even begin to start chipping away at a monstrous national deficit. All the available dollars seem to be getting swallowed up by "other factors."

Oily pocketbooks

Apparently, the world's decision makers started thinking oil provided the fastest way to big bucks status. But somewhere along the long road to secure both the oil and the bucks, a lot of people died.

It's not even fun to begin to think about where all the money is or what is being done with it. Or the oil. Let alone the oil wasted in the 2010 BP catostrophe.

Yet the train of thought seemed to be: disregard the people.

It's wrong.

Nevertheless, in the millennium's crest, false hype suggested a rationing supply of oil problem. A peril that resulted in hikes at the pump and problems with personal pocketbooks. Where do we go from here?

No oil means no travel. No travel means you get no where. Which means no commercialization. No commercialization to function as a society. A simple life in a hectic world never seemed so great. Nicole and Paris, you lived the "Simple Life," why don't you explain?

What a concept. Paris Hilton talking about the simple life of society. Living without money. Now that really is a stretch.

Anyways, back to the oil crisis. It's big. A problem that doesn't necessarily mean damage if kept in perspective. It just scares people. It's a nasty little perk that people in power use to try to make the other side flinch. 'Cuz if you don't have oil, you won't get to work. That could cause problems for a lot of people.

If you don't think the "war on terror" was about money and oil, consider this:

If the United States wasn't concerned about who controlled the world, who had the lion's share of the greatest resources — outside of freedom, of course — then why would the American government be so deep in debt over the expenditures on the war?

A Sept. 27, 2007 article published by McClatchy Newspapers told the story:

The story revealed the Bush Administration requested that Congress increase war spending by $42 billion in 2008. It was an increase that would escalate spending on the war to $189 billion in 2008 alone, and more than $600 billion for the fighting in Iraq since the U.S. invasion was initiated.

War spending in 2008 would reach levels higher than any other year since the fighting broke out in March 2003, the story reported. The Iraq war's spending totals were approaching the 1964-73 estimated total of $518 billion, in 2007 dollars.

On Oct. 24, 2007, the *USA Today* ran a story that revealed the cost of the wars in Iraq and Afghanistan could reach $2.4 trillion by 2010. The estimate included Bush's $46 billion request for additional war spending.

Talk about another horrifying thought. And you don't think the war had anything to do with money and controlling power.

Something suggests the U.S. wouldn't be so concerned with threats if it didn't mean money was at stake for the greatest country in the world to stick its neck on the line for five years and $600 billion. And that didn't even take into consideration, that while millions had been praying — demanding — a ceasefire for years, that no end or peace agreement was in sight.

Yet the U.S. would continue spending money hand over fist, so long as it had control and autonomy to govern society.

Hmm …

In late January of 2007, with the automotive industry in Michigan in utter collapse, gas stations around the Great Lakes made a ploy to slash prices under $2 per gallon in an effort to spur new car sales. The *Detroit Free Press* ran a front page story, questioning whether a drop in pump prices could actually trigger more care sales.

The gimmick didn't last long. Within weeks, prices were over $2 a gallon again, and by April prices were around $2.60 at the pump. In the last week of March, gas prices in the Motor City jumped 10 cents within a couple days.

Needless to say, the war was still going on. President Bush was constantly being criticized. People continued to die, and there was no solution in sight to the oil and gas problems.

That brings us to alternative B.

Electric cars.

Great, a solution. No more gas. No more oil needed to make the car power on and actually allow us to escape somewhere else. Allow us to go to work for a living.

Splendid.

We can actually do our economy some good, save resources, not worry so much about what troops on both sides started fighting over. Really why they began killing other people — yeah, there may be "other motives," but it all boils down to one real thing.

Natural resources.

Something man has put a price tag on.

The Middle East and United States enraptured themselves in this business of natural resources, this battle for power, this so-called concept of freedom, this so-called idea of worshiping one god. But everyone knows, oil was at the crux of the commotion.

The surge in gas prices caused a spike in oil and gas stocks. A book, "Oil Rush of 2006, Top 6 Oil & Gas Stocks" claimed how leading oil and gas companies were recording record profits. In July of 2006, gas prices, in terms of real inflation dollars, were drawing close to an all-time high. People in the gas business take their money seriously. Any false move by an employee giving out a little free gas to his friends was a cardinal sin. One Phoenix, Ariz., man, Duane as he was called, said he was fired for doing just that. Aside from poor decisions on his part as it relates to loyalty to an employer, Duane invested a serious interest in monitoring the gas price structure on a relatively keen level.

It was 2005, and Duane was working for The Home Depot at the time. His days in the gas pump and oil business were over, and he predicted gas prices would spike relatively soon.

By golly, if he wasn't right. If you visited the gas pump in 2006, you'd have thought Duane was damn near genius. Or maybe just someone who studied oil spikes. Either way, he also forecast how there would be spikes in gas prices around the next presidential election, and that incoming nation's leader would then look like a hero when he took the oval office and found a way to shrink dollars at the pump.

So why all this madness over oil in the Middle East? Why the need to make as much money as possible off oil?

So people can get to work?

Governments, both overseas and in the United States, despite their decisions to extend the fighting in Iraq way too long, were asking for support. Sometimes in the form of money.

In the early days of 2007, The USO World Headquarters in Washington, D.C., which claims it is separate from the U.S. government, circulated a letter begging for money. It read:

Winter in Iraq. It's lonely … cold … and still way too dangerous.

Over 150,000 of our GIs, who couldn't get "home for the holidays," are now facing more long months at the Front. They can't feel the warmth of home and family. They can't hug their kids or hear their laughter. Instead, imperiled by unrelenting assaults from a vicious, hidden enemy, they must try their best to prevent a civil war and give a fledgling democracy a fighting chance for survival.

Many of these young troops are weary combat veterans on their second or third tour at the Front. Others are National Guard and Reserve called to active duty, whose families are left to cope without a father, or a mother, or in some cases both. Here at home, the debate drags on over how long they'll have to stay in harm's way; yet over there, they remain dedicated, loyal and professional. So, for as long as they are there, we — the USO — have a mission:

*— **To show our men and women overseas that America still cares ... and that we are grateful for their loyalty and their sacrifice.***

... Please send whatever you can, right away. ...

The message likely was genuine. But without money, without a war over control, without a struggle to determine who owns the most oil, people may not be fighting.

Naturally, fighting was a cause for national criticism. In March of 2007, *CBS* ran an episode on "60 Minutes," questioning some of the tactics used, portrayed on the show as brutal. Women and children were killed in house attacks. Around that time, reports resurfaced about the facts of former NFL player Pat Tillman's death in a shooting in Afghanistan April 22, 2004. Weeks later, controversy began to swirl when the Pentagon notified the Tillman family he died as a result of "friendly fire." The Tillman family and others suggested the Department of Defense delayed details over his death to protect the U.S. armed forces' image. Tillman was initially reported to have been killed by enemy forces. The debate carried on, with more details popping up, television reports later aired with other fighters in his 2nd Ranger Battalion coming forward to provide details into his death. ESPN aired a piece with specific details and comments in the fall of 2006. Tillman's family didn't remain silent, speaking out, a quarter of the way into 2007.

You got the feeling a lot of people were getting tired of the war, and every aspect of it.

Anyways, back to the cars and this problem of penny-pinching at the pump. Here's an idea, why not just make more electric cars? Drop the price on electric cars and produce more of them. While money still exists, just raise the cost for gas-guzzling vehicles. That would encourage others to dismiss the idea of "pumping up" just to go to work.

There you have it. Buy an electric car, forget the war over oil and we'll call it even. Shake hands and call it a truce. You go your way and we'll go ours.

No hard feelings.

A few simple words might facilitate that.

"Sorry," for starters.

Imagine how life could be more peaceful if oil wasn't such a concern. Literally, just put to bed this idea of gas and oil. Let alone water and oil. They don't mix.

BP figured that out the hard way.

Make more cars that don't require using up natural resources. Use the power of one of the most abundant natural resources.

Solar power.

Sunshine.

Whatever, just forget about the oil if it's causing that many problems.

Sound like a plan? Great. Go trade in your car now. Get yourself an electric or solar-powered car. You may even qualify for a tax credit. Just don't be alarmed by the sticker price when you get to the dealership.

It could mean more money up front. That's OK, in the long run, you'll save in gas prices, and that fight for oil will seem more trivial.

Only problem is you can't erase history. The sad part about it is too many lives have been spared. And nothing can be done to change that.

NYC love in tow

Speaking of resources, and how it relates to money, you'd have thought after the problems and drama surrounding New York City and 9-11, the Big Apple would have a sense of compassion to those driving or using gasoline and oil as a means of transportation, especially in and around its own city.

But the empire that is NYC doesn't care.

It simply wants to make money, any way it can.

Need proof? Take for example the way it handles parking around Manhattan and the Bronx. Everyone knows New York is one of the most populated areas in the United States. That means there are lots of cars or other vehicles that enter the city.

New York City's way of looking at that is: more people, more money. One of the methods the city uses to accomplish its money-sucking means is by towing vehicles and then holding the owner of the vehicle ransom until money is exchanged.

Here's how it works.

If you park your car in New York City, a car operated by fuel, it's subject to being snatched.

"All of New York is a tow-away zone," said a female night supervisor at the New York City police department Manhattan tow pound, located near 38th Street and 12th Avenue.

This woman elected to provide only her last name, Bernstein.

All of NYC is a tow-away zone.

If that's the case, everyone in the city of New York better start moving their vehicles into New Jersey or better yet, the Hudson River because their cars are about to be towed.

If a car is towed to the 38th Street and 12th Avenue tow pound, for whatever reason a police officer or city official decides, the owner of the vehicle must find their way to the tow pound. Officers on the street or city officials won't necessarily tell a person all the specifics, just that the person has to pick up his or her car near the Hudson River.

That could mean a nice long walk.

Or a hefty cab fare.

Once arriving at the tow pound, car owners in search of their own property are forced to stand in line just to approach the protective windows, behind which tow pound employees are *sometimes* working. The city of New York has a history of towing a ton of cars, so usually the lines just to approach the window are lengthy. When your turn in line finally reaches the end of the waiting game stage and you hear a, "Next" from a voice behind the windows, it could mean it's your turn to speak. Or it could just mean, you have to listen to what the voice on the other side of the window says, follow "their orders" and then take a seat and wait some more. It doesn't mean it's your turn to get your car back, right then. But you at least have the opportunity to start the process. Of course, you better be the owner of the vehicle or you might have bigger problems getting the car back.

Even if you were the person driving it when it was towed, and the owner is, say, in another state.

Tow pound officials will ask for proof of insurance, proof of identity and registration to the vehicle. Some of that information may be in the vehicle, of course. Some of that information may also be in another state. But the tow pound offers no pity in the case of the latter.

The vehicle is stored on the tow pound's grounds, possibly under a warehouse roof, and in many cases improperly parked, mind you. So if the information the people behind the window are requesting to the vehicle is in the car or not in your possession, and the legal car owner isn't around, it could be a longer process than you, at this point were so ticked off about, let alone hoped for.

"They like it when you're at their mercy," a woman from New York said. "They love it."

Upon acquiring all of the documentation to verify identity and proof of ownership of a vehicle — whether that means flying the owner in from another state or waiting hours for that person to drive into New York, and hope she or he doesn't have a car towed upon arrival — the person being held at the tow pound is then at the city of New York's mercy once again.

"Have a seat and wait for your name to be called," a voice behind the window will say.

Signs are posted on the walls, with improper gramma albeit, that state a person can ask to speak to a supervisor. It doesn't necessarily mean they'll get anywhere with a supervisor, but according to the signs on the walls, people who enter the tow pound's "prison" doors have that right.

After another lengthy wait, as long as the person retrieving the car has proper identification and documentation, he or she is hit with at least a $185 retrieval fee. If the person doesn't have the funds, in forms required by the city of New York, of course, the vehicle is subject to being held on the tow grounds overnight or longer. Each day the car is held results in an additional $20 fee. At least those were the charges levied in early 2007.

That's ridiculous, and even the city officials working at the tow pound won't argue it.

"Why would I think agony is fun?" said Johnny Mitchell, a New York City police department tow pound official who worked at the location near the river.

After paying the $185 fee, the car-operator "criminal" is given slips of paper and another ticket, with more violation fees ranging from $35 to $115, before being directed through a set of wooden stairs mimicking a plank, into a tiny roofed trailer on the tow pound grounds. An official inside that location, seated at a desk, then checks the documents the employees from behind the window give to the "erroneous vehicle operator" after paying the $185. If all inspections and paperwork meet New York City standards, the violators are then told to wait for a van driver to pick them up outside the trailer building.

"It's extortion," a woman from New York said a day after having her car towed from Harlem on Jan. 10, 2007. "Highway robbery. This city should never be in a deficit with this."

After the van driver picks up the person waiting to retrieve his or her vehicle, he or she drives each *violator* to the car that's been towed hours or sometimes days earlier. (Note: the car, still on tow pound property, isn't always parked properly.) If the paperwork matches up according to license plate and documentation, and the person picking up the car has keys to the car, he or she is allowed to take possession of the car.

Whoopee!

But wait, there is another step.

Then the driver has to follow the signs around the tow pound grounds to a booth, where another employee is waiting to verify more information before lifting the rail and allowing the driver to escape into the perilous streets of New York.

Liberty and Justice for all.

"Not here. Not in New York," said Larry McArthy, a New York resident. "It's just about money."

McArthy was helping out a friend who moved from Maryland in early January of 2007. Tow pound officials wouldn't release the car to his friend because she only had a temporary ID card. Yet New York City's tow pound staff charged McArthy's credit card.

In another words, we'll take money, but getting the car back isn't so easy.

Here are what others who experienced the pitfalls of parking in New York have said:

"How you gonna give me a ticket for no bad reason?" complained Rafael Gomez, a York, Penn., resident who had his car towed from a 110th Street and Columbus Avenue location he parked on a routine basis. It was a location other cars have also parked constantly.

"Of course it's all about money."

A CBS television crew worker pleaded with the no first-named Bernstein to have his company vehicle released so he could return to the field. A field that is, notwithstanding, over-the-edge in terms of how it pursues a story. No name Bernstein denied his request. Call that spurning the media.

"There's been tons of stories done on this," the CBS employee said of the perennial parking problems.

Tiffany Ross, of Lawndale, N.C., had her rental car taken from a 26th Street and Broadway location. She, too, was subject to all the tow pound charges.

"The police will stand and watch you park and as soon as you turn your back, they tow it away," Ross said. "It sucks. They're hitting people over the head for money."

Only in New York.

Well, maybe not entirely. Quests for money at the little guy's expense exist everywhere.

"Cities are crazy, and New York is the worst," Friedlander said. "Cities make money off of everything. It goes into the hands of some powerful CEO."

Powerful by greed.

New York resource-full-not or not, there are inadequacies in the way natural resources are used. The sad part is all of those resources were given as a gift from above. For human beings to put a price tag on them seems more than wrong. It seems downright evil.

"I hate how people are using resources to profit off of," said Aggeliki Barberopoulou, a Greece-raised woman who later moved on to work for the University of Southern California's Viterbi School of Engineering as a postdoctoral research associate in the department of civil environmental engineering.

Barberopoulou was also miffed at the Japanese for slaughtering dolphins. She started her own boycott against any Japanese-oriented form of commerce until that Far East culture put an end to their torture to dolphins.

Help me, my health matters

Maybe even scarier to humans is the "torture" it has become to try to stay healthy. Yeah, you all know how difficult it is to schedule a doctor's appointment these days. The first thing a doctor's office wants to know is if you have insurance. After that, then they put you on a waiting list for a month or two before you can make an appointment. By that time, you could be dead.

Seriously, though, to treat a cold, disease or serious health concern with a month's wait time is absolutely ridiculous. Not to mention when you do see a doctor, a lot of times they listen to you for about five minutes and then prescribe a prescription. You know, chemicals, drugs. Something to take the edge off, all the while providing side effects.

By the way, did you know that any time you take antibiotics, your immune system is actually weakening in certain respects? It's true. Your body produces healthy bacteria and bad bacteria. When you take antibiotics, they kill off the good bacteria. You must take probiotics, acidophilus or bifidus, specifically a human grade bifidus, to neutralize the effects of antibiotics that destroy your body's natural ability to produce good bacteria.

Anyways, back to the doctor office disasters. Denzel Washington's "John Q" movie told it all. If you don't have insurance, if you can't pay the big bucks, we can't treat you. That's how it's gotten nowadays. For anything really. No money, no service.

That is sad. Especially when it comes to your health and saving lives.

"I think the only doctors worth seeing nowadays are surgeons," said Robert, a Russian barber living in the United States. "Doctors will see you for five minutes and then tell you to go buy a prescription."

Precisely prescribed.

That is, if you have the money to pay for it.

In-debt-ed to money

It's became glaring how unfair money had become to most people when you consider the numbers behind the system in place.

On January 23, 2007, *USA Today* ran an editorial on the Federal deficit. The editorial claimed President George W. Bush was expected to call for balanced budget by 2012 in his State of the Union address, which incidentally he would deliver on the night the *USA Today* story hit newstands. The editorial stated Bush turned the Bill Clinton presidency era surpluses into six straight years of deficits, putting the nation nearly $3 trillion deeper in debt.

In March of 2006, Congress passed a bill by a 52-48 vote that would allow the nation's debt to reach $9 trillion. Congress is made up of both the Democratic and Republic parties, mind you.

In its editorial, *USA Today* argued, "now is not the time to ballyhoo the potential for a balanced budget in 2012. It is the time to address health care costs, which rise by 10% to 15% in most years. It is also the time to fix Social Security and enact policies that encourage people to work longer."

Things had gotten so bad in the U.S. economy that in September of 2007, an *Associated Press* story revealed the Federal Reserve bank added billions of more dollars to the banking system in a battle to prevent the credit crisis affecting the dwindling U.S. dollar and its subsequent economy from reaching a complete collapse.

Here's a suggestion, why not just eliminate money, and that would eliminate all those concerns. Including the national debt.

Which, by the way, reportedly climbed past $7 trillion on January 15, 2004. The outstanding public debt was reported at $8,753,333,042,064.25 on Feb, 21, 2007. The estimated population of the United States was reported as 301,010,578. Divide the debt by each person, and guess what?

We're all looking at a share of $29,079.82 in debt.

Sound good to you?

Chapter 2

Education, edification & ethics ... eerie

S hall we examine ethics in education? Or maybe more appropriate, inflation in education?

When you consider the rising cost of education, it's hard to gauge whether educators really have their true interest on the students or fattening their pocketbooks. Of course, educators and school legislators are not the only people dictating why education costs are so high.

Guess that's why people say it's all about the mighty dollar these days. And that's surely the case when it comes to going to school.

To attend Lehigh University in 2006-07 students would see bills totalling somewhere in the neighborhood of $44,700. At Harvard, it was between $46,450 and $48,850.

In 1995, one credit hour for part-time graduate students at the University of Notre Dame was a shade under $1,000. Eleven years later, in that same educational scenario, semester credit hour tuition costs ran roughly $1,822. Former Fighting Irish students and South Bend, Ind., newspaper editors used to joke about how much they paid for a Notre Dame education only to wind up reading news copy in ... South Bend.

"Look where it's got us," wisecracked Ken Bradford, a former University of Notre Dame student who later served as an editor at the *South Bend Tribune*.

Years removed from his own schooling, Bradford dismissed the idea of a graduate student wanting to attend Notre Dame.

"Three thousand dollars for one class?" Bradford said, dumbfounded at the thought. "That's a nice down payment on a house."

In the 2006-07 school year, on-campus full-time undergraduate international students at UCLA were paying $25,825 in university-assessed fees. That didn't include room and board. Add those two costs into the equation and those particular Bruin students were looking at a bill of roughly $42,725. Plus, there were $4,500 spouse visa and $2,000 additional funds per child fees for the international students. For California residents, costs were estimated at $16,219 if the students were living with relatives or $23,392 if they were living in residence halls. Every student was required to pay a $619 health insurance fee.

The University of Minnesota's per credit costs were $291.85 for resident undergrads and 739.15 for non-residents in 2006-07. Multiply those figures by a full-time class load of 15 credits — and remember these were just tuition costs — and Gopher resident and non-resident students were baited into bills of $4,377.75 and $11,087.25, respectively. That didn't include living expenses or books.

In the late 80s, early 90s, tuition costs for an in-state undergraduate student at Western Michigan University were $65 per credit hour. By 2007, those fees had risen to $215 per hour. Graduate students at small, primarily locally-known Pennsylvania schools were paying $360 per credit hour in 2007. That's a thousand bucks per class. That's where Notre Dame was 12 years earlier.

Amazing.

Western Michigan University's interim president Diether Haenicke explained why universities keep raising costs. He cited increased costs levied by outside agencies, not enough funding from the state government, routine staff threats to strike and on and on and on. He was tired of explaining it.

You begin to wonder whether the educational system's rise in costs is more about inflation or inflated pocketbooks.

Or greed.

"Hallelujah," Haenicke said Jan. 8, 2007. "That's exactly it. People just don't know when to stop. The greed is increasing in the world."

Not everyone has greedy intentions. But there sure is a heck of a lot of it. And it's no different as it relates to education.

Haenicke, Western Michigan's fifth president, had served as the school's leading figure from 1985 to 1998. He also was academic vice president of Wayne State University and Ohio State University. Western Michigan beckoned back the German-born scholar in August of 2006 when one of his predecessors, a female president who lasted only three years at the school, resigned.

Haenicke's thoughts and comments on rising education costs came two days after the football team for the university he was representing at the time lost by three points in the first NCAA bowl game played outside the United States since 1937. It was the same day the football team from a previous employer, the school in Columbus, Ohio, was run over in the first ever BCS National Championship, ruining an unbeaten season.

Bowl games, by the way, are big business. A lot of money circulates around college football bowl games. Some college football players spoke publicly in the 2006-07 bowl season about how they should be entitled to receive a piece of the bowl game's profits since they were the athletes that risked their bodies to generate all the money. Forget about just playing the sport and trying to win the game. Not to mention the free education they likely received for suiting up in pads from mid-August until Jan. 1. Nowadays, athletes — former University of

Michigan basketball player Chris Webber was accused of it, too, in the early 90s — are commonly buying into the "dollar days" of college life. But accepting money, gifts and favors, although it goes on all the time at the collegiate level, is illegal for college athletes. At least according the NCAA.

Anyways, Haenicke questioned why he would be asked to speak on the concept of money. He made succinct comments about how he brought in little income. Maybe little in the big picture. Surely when you consider that just five days earlier The Home Depot CEO Bob Nardelli was awarded a severance package worth $210 million following his resignation after six years at the helm of the world's largest home improvement store chain, an interim university president's pay may be peanuts. Nardelli's resignation was prompted because he was criticized for laying claims to enormous paychecks and the company's poor stock performance.

Hmm, issues both heavily based on money.

Haenicke's comments also came a week after Miami Dolphins coach Nick Saban bolted the NFL for the University of Alabama, securing a guaranteed eight-year contract worth $32 million plus $700 to $800 thousand in bowl game bonuses. Saban, a former college coach at Michigan State and Louisiana State, returned to the NCAA game shortly after he made comments that were replayed over and over again about his disinterest in the Alabama job. He had not fulfilled his commitment to

Dolphins multi-billion dollar owner Wayne Huizenga, also the leading figure of Blockbuster and AutoNation, the nation's largest automotive dealer. Huizenga was creator of three Fortune 500 companies and voted Financial World Magazine's CEO of the Year five times and a 2005 recipient of Ernst & Young World Entrepreneur of the Year.

But one man's interest said so long to an expert entrepreneur. Huizenga reportedly gave Saban his blessings to leave after hearing the coach and his wife's rationale. Saban's Dolphin Dash signalled greed in a few different ways. Not including the cash. He wanted, as many people do, to do what mattered most to him and his wife, instead of honoring a commitment to others, in this case Huizenga and his team.

All this talk of money circulating around the world within such a minute class of people, in such a short period of time, was sickening to a university president. Haenicke, who originally retired but was bugged to come back by WMU after a 13-year presidency, spoke publicly that he wished the university would identify its candidate quickly to take over the presidency so he could return to a retirement lifestyle he was enjoying with his wife Carol.

After all, who would want to be swallowed up in money talk and all that educational baggage after you already exited stage left?

"These are the things that are just obscene," Haenicke said of the aforementioned stories relating to money and the educational business' role with it. "Yeah, it's crazy. We have really struggling families trying to pay for their kids' education. I just hate to see it."

He mimicked, almost disgustingly, at the idea of other students attending schools such as Harvard, Notre Dame or Lehigh because of those institutions high-priced cost factor. Yet he realized that even the school he was representing was asking too much for students to try to prepare for a future.

"We are a real bargain at Western Michigan," he said, "but even a being a real bargain has become a struggle to many students."

Wonder what the kids who chose Lehigh, Harvard and Notre Dame think?

Lehigh's administration elected not to comment on the issue.

On April 16, 2007, the nation's eyes were glued to Virginia Tech. Seung-Hui Cho, a student at the school in Blacksburg, Va., gunned down 30 people and injured 15 others inside Norris Hall, an engineering building on campus. Two others were shot and killed in a dormitory. He later took his life when police converged on him.

Cho, a 23-year-old Asian student who killed two victims who attended the same high school he did, Westfield High School in Chantilly, Va., revealed clues in a video CD that was sent to NBC's headquarters in New York. His message offered clues as to what his motives were in performing the deadliest mass killings in U.S.

history. He suggested he was treated unfairly by other students, and targeted rich students who drove Mercedes and had plenty of money in his attacks.

"All your debaucheries weren't enough," Cho said via the video sent to NBC. "I didn't have to do this. I could've left. I could've fled. But no, I will no longer run. You have vandalized my heart. Thanks to you, I die like Jesus Christ."

Sad, but true, money and people's "status" apparently played a role in the Virginia Tech massacre.

Even high schools are affected by money, sometimes drastically. And that doesn't just include schools that charge their students to walk through the doors. In other words, those schools that operate on tuition.

Surely, you've heard of teachers are asking for more money or else … In the second week of January 2007, the *New York Post* ran a story headlined, "N.Y. risks losing fed bucks for education." The story reported how the state could lose millions of dollars in federal education aid unless all New York state teachers met qualifying standards. The article went on to report in New York City 87 percent of classroom teachers met the requirements in 2006, an improvement of nearly nine percent from the previous year.

Yet almost one in five science and reading classes and nearly one in every three art courses were taught in New York City public schools by teachers without enough "qualifications" in those respective areas. A teachers union president credited salary hikes for retaining instructors. In some ways, that could be translated: "pay us more and we'll get ourselves qualified."

A Nashville area teacher, Steve Goodpaster, had three children. Before his kids even became teenagers, he and his wife told them they could live at home as long as they wanted. Thoughts of sending his kids to college wasn't any different than most people — a concern. Especially considering the escalating education costs.

Many students are going into college life with good intentions: they want to learn. But they're getting stuck with big bills when they come out.

"Now it's becoming really hard for people to come out and pay back that money," Goodpaster said.

Oh really.

Alma mater allegiance

Jamie Jeremy, an executive director of an alumni relations department for Western Michigan University, confirmed the school she represented hauled in millions of dollars each year.

Just in donations.

She didn't have the exact figure, acknowledged that she should know that, but confirmed it was in the millions.

"While money is important to the alumni association, we have bills to pay," Jeremy said. "We look to the alumni to become members and dues paying members."

In other words, give your alma mater money, and you'll be considered an alumnus with a gold star. Part of the club. Before the start of the 2007 new year, the alumni association Jeremy spearheaded sent out brochures, urging former Western Michigan students to make New Year's resolutions. The brochure read:

New Year's Resolutions
1) Cut the Calories
2) Cut the Carbs
3) Cut the Check to Western Michigan University every year!

About a month after those cards were sent out, Jeremy attempted to clarify her statements about WMU alumni association's goal. She insisted it isn't always about the money. But it really is.

"We deal in two currencies," Jeremy tried to reason. "The currency that is almost as important to me is the time and energy."

Notice how she said, "*almost*."

Precisely.

Time and energy is *almost* as important as the actual almighty dollar. But neither the educational system nor the government recognize "time" and "energy" with a definitive equation for compensation. Not now anyway.

In other words, those "currencies" hold no value compared to money. Jeremy knew it. She just may not have straightened out her own thoughts clearly to internally rationalize it herself. Of course, that's not to single her out. Some people who hold positions of authority aren't always the sharpest tools in the shed either.

"For as hard as it is to write a 5-, 10-, 15-, 30-dollar membership dues check, it's just as hard for them to put in the time," Jeremy said ... "because they're working three minimum wage jobs to exist."

Uh huh.

Struggling to survive. A life that begins after school. In some cases, a school bought at a pretty penny.

A school whom students paid a pretty penny to buy an education they believed would earn them more money.

Chapter 3

Buying into banking

I t's starting to become a stretch whether banks are major culprits contributing to the money problems or just main cogs in the equation that cause so many individuals problems.

Or is it really the actual money makers and those "in power" themselves?

Or are customers — individuals living their lives, trying to get by — just always guilty of wrongdoings, therefore warranting fees and creating their own problems because they're just a menace to the banking society? That pretty much covers the whole world.

With a devilish influence, of course.

Either way, the whole idea of banking is a sore spot to many people when it comes to all the baggage that goes along with a person's wealth. Not to mention status, and what they do for a living. Banks, financial institutions, credit unions, they're all required to report money to the federal government.

Scary thought huh?

"It's the law," Bullard said. "It's what we do."

Bullard, a big-time supporter of credit unions, citing they were formed on the basis of cooperatives, believed in her line of work. It's the reason she became a CEO. But she also knows at what cost people will go to secure money.

"There's nothing more dear to people than their money," Bullard said.

Why is that? Why is money so near and dear to people? Could it be there's so much emphasis put on money, and the need to survive today depends on riches to do anything?

As money grows for one party, so it balloons or suffocates for another. Banks often become beneficiaries. The bigger the bank, the better the chance the majority will be swallowed up.

Majority meaning you and your neighbor.

"I know that I've belonged to a bank in the past and I've felt like a number," Bullard said.

Banks, financial institutions, places that hold your money and make more for themselves off of it, operate under a "make sure we get ours" mentality first. The whole idea is to take a little more if need be, and then see if you can actually help the little guys when the time is right. At least that's the way the bank's mind seemingly operates.

They say everyone is in business to make money. Not all people succeed. So when a loss sets in, it's often times looked at as just that — a loss. Oh well, chalk that one up as a loss. Move on.

Problem is, the way the current system is set up not many people can just move on. It's what we call hardship, and there is plenty of it in the world as it exists today.

Bank policies enforce a wait time for funds to clear. Especially for new bank customers. After people deposit checks, they are often times subject to the bank's disgression as to when the funds will clear. Different banks have different hold time periods, some as lunatic-like long as nine days. Wachovia was notorious for those ridiculously-long strangleholds. Other banks may hold funds for two or three days. To you as an individual, that essentially means you must sit back and wait to see when you are free to spend your own money.

It has gotten out of hand.

But it's the *bank's* or *financial institution's* rules.

Just don't forget, "money is near and dear to everyone." Especially the people it rightfully belongs to.

With holds, banks often use a smokescreen to present their rationale for why it's OK to take money from you, but then not release it until a certain time. They present this business of "funny business." In other words, there's a lot of paranoia involved. Banks often use the "money fraud" rationalization in defense. But with bills never ceasing, with every company — the government included — always begging for money, and very few companies willing to work with you when you're in a bind, people just don't have time to wait.

Well, if there wasn't money, there wouldn't be any fraud.

The whole idea of someone going into another person's account to take money is a sick thought indeed. But maybe banks, if they want to continue to buy into this concept of money, need to find ways to safeguard against having to put unnecessary holds on honest, true and forthright citizens' accounts when they need to access their own funds.

A 90-day period to "get to know you," or "form a relationship" is jargon. Just a bank's way of saying, "keep the money in our hands for a while, and we'll be nice to you." It's wrong. A person's money, if this truly were a society that allows freedom, should be a person's money. Not a person's money under certain conditions.

But that's the way the banks have it set up.

Let's use an example. A woman moves from Montana to Louisiana. She wants to escape the natural beauty and cold for a lifestyle around Mardi Gras. Hootin' and hollerin' all the time. No more serenity. An all-about-the-cash and party lifestyle.

OK, it's her choice. That is the basis of America, right? Freedoms, the pursuit of happiness and guidelines our forefathers laid out to begin our country with honest, governing practices.

So she packs up her materialistic belongings and loads them up in the car and rental truck, which costs her $2,347 to move — her own possessions, mind you — from one state to another with some miles in between. All right. Three days, two hotel nights and a lot of real estate covered on the road later, she's in Louisiana. Closer to the action. All the excitement. Nightlife. Partying. Money-chasing activities.

Yeah.

Next step for this woman is to situate in a place and deposit some money into an account. She closed her account in Montana because the inconvenience of keeping it open was just too overbearing, no matter how much the bank just outside of Missoula tried to convince her that everything would be all right. The staff there tried to tell her just to leave the funds in her account, and they'd take care of everything for her.

But she was a little leery about that because the inconvenience of ATM fees was a little nonsensical to her. And moving to a different location would mean she wouldn't have access to the ATMs in Montana. She knew what that meant: a bank would find ways to "bank" some of her money just because she decided to withdraw cash from her own account. It was quite an absurd concept, she thought. Plus, the idea of depositing out-of-state checks with nine-day holds placed on them wasn't appealing to her either. Not when her funds weren't blessed with enough Benjamin Franklin insignias. She was used to seeing more George Washingtons, Abraham Lincolns and, occasionally, Andrew Jacksons. Besides, the company she lined up employment with a little outside of New Orleans was going to pay her only after an evaluation period. So gaining access to her money was important.

Important because bill seekers weren't going to give her any breaks.

Car payments. A house that she needed to pay another couple notes on in Montana before new occupants took over. Insurance. None of them were going away, let alone going to give her a grace period. Not a chance. How could a big company afford to let the little guy slide for a little while? They needed to continue to collect.

Collect and fatten their pocketbooks. It's not only the American way. It's society's way.

Problem was, once she arrived in New Orleans, all the banks in and around the Cajun lifestyle, and all banks in every other state for that matter, didn't seem to want to cooperate. They wanted to keep her money for a while before they allowed her to pay her bills.

"Ma'am, once you place your $2,500 into an account here, there will be a 90-day evaluation period. We'll examine your deposit habits. Are you planning on putting more money into the account soon? Do you have more money that you can allow us to consolidate with a savings-checking package? We'll give you a 0.5 percent interest rate if you open another savings account."

In other words, put more money in, allow us to hold onto it for a while, don't panic when you've got bills to pay, and we'll hold onto the funds until we say they're available for your release. But it is your money. And your money is safe with us.

Once your green fattens our green, we'll give you the green light (a few days later, of course) to access a portion of your funds.

Wachovia, surely you know about this concept?

C'mon. A person's money is a person's money. Banks want to present this paranoia fraud front, try to discourage their customers from spending any of their funds, regardless if they have bills to pay or need food to eat, to keep the funds wrapped up in their house for as long as possible before releasing it to the rightful owners or other companies.

Companies that are begging, prodding and reaching for that same person's funds in order to widen their pockets.

It's an unfair system. It stinks. And the banks themselves know it. Some of them favor it, some bank employees agree it's wrong what they do. If money must exist, if banks must exist, why not just one bank?

"I agree with you," Alex Angulo, a Phoenix banking center specialist, confessed on a late January 2007 day.

Banks are known for commonly placing holds on out-of-state checks. They charge ridiculous fees, even if you overdraw your account by a penny. And they yearn for customers to put their money into checking accounts. Because that's where they make the majority of their profits.

"Banks make their money off the fees they charge," Angulo said.

Angulo confirmed banks want customers to open checking accounts more than any other account because that's where a financial institution such as the one he worked for profits most. Checking accounts often have many stipulations, requirements and bank-enforced "rules."

Banks know a lot of people can't adhere to those "rules," let alone maintain minimum balances, have spending needs, not to mention habits, of their own. They are fully aware that these accounts will be overdrawn or drop below balance requirements, which, for these financial instutions, means more money for them.

A noble concept: making money off of something another person *doesn't* have.

Don't bank on it

Sometimes banks will tell you one thing and do another.

Case in point, an employee from LaSalle Bank, an institution run by Norman Bobbins, told a customer who deposited $20,000 into a certificate of deposit account in 2006, there would be no penalties on withdrawals from the

CD prior to the maturation date. The customer was told by a LaSalle Bank employee a penalty would only be levied on the interest accrued at the time of any early withdrawals.

If you can understand where the bank was going with that convoluted no-fees, only-fees-in-certain-cases conundrum.

Three months into the CD's term, a period that was set up to mature in four months, the customer needed to access some of the funds within the CD account to pay bills, in large part due to circumstances in which other people put him in a bind. At that point, the CD had generated $203.90 in interest. That meant the customer's account had grown to 20,203.90. According to what the customer was told upon placing the funds into LaSalle Bank's hands, a penalty on the $203.90 is all that should have been instituted. Maybe $50, maybe $100. Heck even if LaSalle elected to take the entire amount of the interest earned that would mean the bank would pocket a little over $200. Instead, LaSalle hit the customer with a $436.93 early withdrawal penalty the day after the CD account was opened up for him to draw funds from.

A difference of $640.83.

Greed, you say?

Forget the concept of interest. Banks are just looking for ways to acquire more money, and LaSalle was certainly guilty of that in this instance. LaSalle went back on its word. It made false promises.

It robbed the customer of his own money.

For no reason other than greed.

LaSalle was part of the ABN Amro Group. Its banks were formerly umbrellaed under the Standard Federal name. Bobbins, its esteemed chairman, enjoyed touting LaSalle as the second largest bank in the Chicago region after starting out as a just baby financial center.

In 2007, Bobbins' public relations staff declined interviews in regards to bank policies and questions about money. After being pulled out of a meeting, Shaun Platt, a LaSalle Bank public relations specialist, turned phone media requests over to associate Brad Krieger, who in turn requested media inquisitions be made through e-mail correspondence. Krieger never responded, nor acknowledged the e-mails until a subsequent phone call was made. At that point, Krieger claimed without specifying reasons, "We cannot grant that request."

"You can't or you won't?" Krieger was pressed.

"Both."

In other words, questions about money and banks just don't coincide. Not according to Krieger anyway.

Krieger was obviously annoyed at handling the job he was hired to do, handling a media request. The president of his company may have never even been made aware of attempts from the media to contact him. Frankly, LaSalle and other big wigs from major corporations or schools seeking the big bucks, didn't want to talk about money or the problems surrounding it because they were getting their share of it. Why should the system change for them? They were making tons of money. They like it the way it is.

Here is what Bobbins said of his bank in earlier reports:

"In 1980 you could not find LaSalle Bank in anyone's statistics, as we were so small. In 2000, we are the No. 2 bank in the city. We have come a long way because we have had a strategy and we have stuck to it. We know where we want to go, and we have been very focused."

Focused on taking people's money after promising one thing and doing another.

At the time of Bobbins' comments, LaSalle had "banked" its 17th consecutive year of record earnings. Around that time, Bank One chairman James Dimon was in competition, you might say, with Bobbins. Bank One Corporation, which later became Chase Bank, was lauded as America's fifth largest bank. Chicago was an area where the banking business was big business.

"Creativity has always been a big part of financial services, and Chicago has been a hotbed of originality during the past 20 years," Dimon once said.

LaSalle was obviously crafty in finding ways to make money. Even when it meant wrongfully taking money away from customers. Especially after assurances were made to guarantee otherwise.

Bobbins later retired, and LaSalle merged with Bank of America.

Fretting over the fees

When it comes to bank "issues," in other words when an argument ensues because of unexpected fees, all hell breaks loose.

Banks search for ways to issue fines all the time. And the employees who work for the banks won't deny it.

"You got Chase or you got ... They're worth millions of dollars, and they're able to make transactions all the time because they can," said Pam Hill, a guest relations employee for Chase Bank in Texas.

In 2002, Compass Bank administered $32 fees per item for insufficient funds. By 2006, those fees climbed to $36. Compass Bank disclosures stated they could zap an individual with six (6) insufficient funds charges per day for differing overdraft instances. That meant if any account fell below zero by a penny on one charge, the customer would be responsible for paying $32.01 back. Multiply that by six and a customer is staring at a nasty negative balance at the break of dawn the next day. Compass also had a policy that charged its bankers $25 for every stop payment request. Meaning if a customer asked for a stop payment on a check that had been written, even if after the bank began zapping the customer with six insufficient fees on any given day, the customer would be subject to another $25 penalty.

USA Today ran a front page story on July 9, 2009, headlined, "*Banks get rich on overdraft fees*." The story's subhead, appearing below a $10 bill graphic mounted with a red, white and black "YOUR PENALTY $35.00" stamp over the Hamilton spot, read: *'Courtesy loans at soaring rates draw complaints from consumers.'*

Here's how the lead of the story read:

Even as regulators crack down on abusive mortgage and credit card practices, another type of lending threatens to mire consumers in a credit trap.

It's called "courtesy overdraft," and has long been used by banks to automatically pay transactions that account holders don't have the money to cover — and then charge them a steep fee. For years, banks have made it easier for customers to overdraw their checking accounts, aided by a cottage industry of consultants who make big money by helping to wring fees out of consumers, a USA Today analysis finds.

But what began as a customer service has often become an important revenue driver for banks at the expense of the most vulnerable consumers, according to bank memos reviewed by USA Today and interviews with industry insiders.

"This practice has gone awry and needs to be fixed," says Alex Sheshunoff, a key consultant who once advised banks to pay, not return, overdrawn transactions. "This is something everyone should be trying to find a solution to, not fighting."

Here's a solution: dump this idea of money. Then we won't worry about overdraft fees. Heck, we won't worry about any fees. Let the contributions of society lend itself a helping hand by allowing everyone to pitch in and become entitled to equality. Those who don't pitch in, don't get to share in the equilibrium way of life.

It really is simple.

Indeed banks have the idea of "when it rains, it pours" down pat. They keep pouring it on the customers.

On Sept. 18, 2006, a female posted the following complaint against Compass Bank on a site called CreditSuit.org:

Unfortunately, my husband and I have had the same problem with Compass. It really started when I added him on my account. We have been getting NSF charges up the wazoo, and we don't know why because we balance our checkbook regularly and watch what we spend. A few months ago, my husband was charged double at a restaurant (two totally different amounts, I might add). So, we went to dispute the amount that was not practical. We went through a representative, and she told us specifically what to do and to sign the form, and she sent it in to corporate. Well, I got a letter back from customer service who was handling it, and she said there was not enough information on it. Wait, wasn't this done with the help of someone that knew what to do? I guess not! We have been hit with several 36 dollar charges. Now, I just looked on my bank account and saw six $36 NSF charges totaling $180!! Here's the deal, we put in $600 in cash on 9/11. On 9/12, these charges came about!

What is wrong? What happened? I hate Compass and want to dispute.

In addition to other fees, Compass lists a $20 per hour fee for what they classify as "Research." Such a service charge was applicable to all accounts, according to Compass Bank disclosures.

What?

Research fees?

What the heck is that?

Heaven forbid a bank employee would ever have to conduct research. Even research to discover whether the bank itself committed an error.

A $20 per hour research fee?

If ever there was a case of greed, that was it.

Hey Compass, research this:

In 2004, a female Compass Bank employee told a male banker if the banker ever moved out of state he could keep his account open and mail in deposits, in addition to having direct deposits set up. On-line bill pay was an option, and banking could be conducted as usual.

In the summer of 2006, the same customer was told by a different Compass Bank female employee he could not keep the account open if he moved out of state. The man was planning an out-of-state move, so he had most of his money withdrawn and safely deposited into another financial institution. When the customer arrived at the Compass Bank he'd done the majority of his banking with for the past couple years to close his account, the branch employees pleaded with him to keep the account open. They told him he could keep the account open, and apologized for whatever information he was given by any other Compass employees. He'd made up his mind at that point, based on the information the second female employee told him. He'd already begun the process to simplify his funds into one account. This trip to the bank was to take out the remaining funds to use for the move.

A couple months later, a Compass bank branch manager in Phoenix, told the same customer over the phone he could open another account and maintain the same terms and treatment he had while banking with Compass the past few years. Everything was contingent on him coming into her branch and depositing at least $25. The account he closed a couple months earlier was still pulling up in the bank's computer system at the time of the phone conversation. His account gave glowing marks to the bankers, meaning the customer had a good "relationship" with Compass. That's why Compass employees there — from a teller at the same Phoenix branch to the boss of that branch — made friendly comments about servicing the customer to his banking needs. The customer, who, once again, had moved out of state, didn't act right away. But by the end of the year, he found himself in that branch after travelling across the country, ready to deposit funds and assume the same good-natured terms he had while banking with Compass for several years.

Because they were promised to him by the female branch manager of that Phoenix Compass location.

However, when the customer proceeded to deposit funds into a new account, he was told those good terms had gone bye-bye. He would be subject to holds on deposits, especially when dealing with checks originating from out of state, etc., etc., etc.

Another fine example of a bank telling a customer what they wanted to hear, but acting in an entirely different manner. Despite the fact the customer travelled across the country to open an account based on the terms promised to him by the branch manager. The same branch manager, who when the issue of resolving this mess came up in a separate phone conversation, told the customer she had customers to attend to.

Yet the customer she was talking to, one that had banked with that same location for a few years and developed a "good relationship," wasn't a customer?

Infuriating the investors

Bank employees find ways to turn issues or disputes against the customer many a time. Even when they, the bank employees, know it's their company's fault. Sometimes that's just a case of an employee — and customer service representatives are often guilty of it, too — taking things too personally. Instead of looking at the situation as the customer simply being frustrated with company policy, customer service representatives, bank tellers, telephone bankers and the like often personalize the issue.

Sometimes they do it intentionally, out of spite because they sense hostility. Many of them realize the customers are going to become upset, if not flat out perturbed, when they, as workers, assume a personal stance while also siding with company policies. The worst part about all of it is those employees still want to make it a personal crusade to battle the voice on the other end of the phone or the face on the other side of the counter.

Instead of helping.

Bank employees are big-time guilty of this. And their employer allows them to get away with it. Yet all the fingers are pointed at the customer. That's why customers get so bent out of shape with customer service representatives, tellers or telephone bankers. It's also why customers tell those service industry people to get bent.

"I've been sworn at. I've had people angry at me," said David, a Pioneer Mortgage lending specialist living in Toronto who worked for a company whose headquarters were based in Illinois. "I hate these calls. When you come on the phone, it tells me what to say. I basically do everything off e-mail."

Hmm.

Isn't it funny how companies tell you they don't have the capability to e-mail you when their own company employees have access to e-mail? Isn't it funny how they can write notes about you, but not show you what they're inputting into their system? Isn't it funny how a company tells their lowly-paid customer service reps what to say?

David didn't have a car at the time. He struggled under the current currency system. Even living in Canada. He knew all about the banks. He knew all about Royal Bank. It is one of 13 banks in Canada, and was considered the largest.

He had a great deal of familiarity with the Canadian currency system also. He had to. Lending and money was his line of work.

"It's all regulated by the government," he explained of the Canadian currency system. "The banks are mammoth. They're monster size."

Monster, meaning they've brought in lots of funds and kept smaller banks out of business. If there must be banking, it's actually a noble concept. Really, why can't there be just one bank? One bank consolidated under one name instead of all these competitors who turn profit-seeking measures, the inability to get along with others in the same workforce and greed into a problem for everybody else?

Yes, banks have made mistakes by lending too much money out to people in hopes of turning around a profit, but when society's inequities caused foreclosures on homes and the bank felt it was the one getting robbed because it wasn't getting a return on the funds it allocated, people's possessions started getting taken away. None of it would've happened if greed on everyone's part didn't enter the picture.

Don't need a bigger house. Don't need more toys. Don't need more money. Don't need to borrow to get bigger. Don't need to lend money out to try to pocket more for ourselves. Don't need to go after the big deals so we can fatten our pocket books.

Just need to sit still and enjoy life.

Maybe Bank of America had it right in the current system in the United States. One roof to hold everyone's funds. If there must be money, it's a start.

One bank that stands for freedom of one nation.

One nation which is all about money.

But it would work better when people, bank employees included, subside in their efforts not to bicker. Even those at Bank of America, especially when it regards money. Otherwise, eventually some of those bickering brothers and sisters start a movement to open their own bank. Can't get along with another employee. Don't like the customers you're dealing with because the bank you're employed by has rules that tick the customers off who aren't afraid to tell you.

No problem, just go to the next cubicle down, grab a few employee friends and open your own bank.

Building a bank.

Another noble idea.

One that results in competition and lots of inconveniences. Especially for the individual.

Busting the banks

They say the American dollar is worth an awful lot more than many countries' currencies. That's why people are moving to the United States.

Bardah and Bujar Toska moved their family to the United States from Albania around the turn of the century. A family of four, they eventually settled into the sunny climate of Phoenix.

They, like many Americans, were faced with the same pressures of paying bills to maintain their modest lifestyle in a comfortable house. Bardah, a kind educated woman, friendly neighbor and good citizen, worked in a hospital. Her husband, too, was kind, always offered positive words to others, and their two kids were happy and fun-loving. They made occasional trips back to their homeland when school was out in the summer and the desert heat of Phoenix became a melting pot the same way the U.S. debt burned coals for many people.

Bardah said she brought her family to the country to get a good education, but there weren't too many other things they cared for. One being the scary nature of society's greed and how much money U.S. companies tried to get away with charging people. Her husband became equally frustrated when trying to communicate with companies who rightfully did him wrong.

They spoke about how greed and the chase for money was as prevalent in Albania as it was in America.

"It's everywhere," Bardah said of the dash for cash.

Problem is, there's only so much of it to go around.

In 2007, one U.S. dollar was worth 100.62 Albanian lek.

As the month of January 2007 came to a close, one Japanese Yen held a value of .00821693 when exchanged for an American dollar. That meant one American dollar was worth roughly 121.65 yen.

The euro represented the currency for 13 European countries, including Belgium, Germany, Greece, Spain, the Netherlands, Austria, Portugal, Slovenia, Finland, France, Ireland, Italy and Luxembourg. One euro held the equivalent of 1.293 dollars.

In other words, the almighty U.S. dollar wasn't so mighty. Case in point, in late April of 2007, a man took $125 in cash to Ireland. When he exchanged his U.S. dollars for the European currency, he received 89 euros in return.

Purchasing power

According to MeasuringWorth.com, in 2005, if you were shopping with $23.09 in U.S. dollars, you would have had the same purchasing power as $1 when Ben Franklin, Thomas Jefferson, John Hancock and the like were blueprinting the Declaration of Independence back in 1776. A thousand bucks in 1975 had a value of $3,627.41 three decades later.

Inflation, you say?

In 2007, the inflation rate was slightly over 3 percent. Three doesn't seem to be a high number, but when you compound that over 10 or 20 years and inflation escalates, there are problems.

"You need to keep inflation in check," Baltin said.

Now that's an understatement.

Yet the government or *dollar control department*— and those terms are used loosely— isn't doing it. Inflation continues to climb, people continue to lose jobs, others are struggling on street corners or park benches and a select few keep cashing in on coin.

Federal debts multi-trillion excess translated this way in The *Arizona Republic's* front page headline originating from a Gannett Newspaper sister *USA Today* story on May 29, 2009:

Feds' debt: $547K per household

All of that meant taxpayers were on the hook for an extra $55,000 per household to cover escalating federal commitments made in 2008 to be allocated to retirement benefits. The 12 percent spike in red ink that year was the result of federal borrowing during the recession, coupled with growing costs for Medicare and Social Security.

Two other touchy subjects altogether.

Nonetheless, this story surfaced at a time General Motors went public about bankruptcy issues, while numerous other companies were opting out by selling out and closing their doors.

Sad.

Isn't it amazing that when times became so desperate, people allowed other people to give up and fend for themselves with nothing.

The world would be a better place fending for itself without money. It would be ...

heavenly.

While on a radio show based out of North Hollywood, Calif., Ru Mills, also known as Rayelan Allan, who wrote a book called, "Diana Queen of Heaven," exploring the death of Princess Diana in 1997, had selective words about America's central bank.

"We are collaterals of the Federal Reserve," Mills said. "They milk us."

Commercializing banks

People who've worked for banks have left banking industry careers for that reason. A man from the Dallas area left a career in banking, somewhat prematurely by traditional retirement standards, partly because he didn't like what was going on in the industry. He expressed his distaste for what banks were doing to customers, despised the fees they were implementing and became soured simply talking about being caught up in the "corporate world."

E-Trade ran commercials during Super Bowl 41's (to stick to American numerals) broadcast insinuating just what the former banker was miffed over.

"Don't let your bank rob you," the commercial suggested after a bank manager, masked as a robber, instructed a slew of bankers to hit the floor.

HSBC bank aired a commercial of its own.

"Let your money grow."
"We've found a way to make money get bigger."
(As dollar bills floated into an animated piggy bank centered on the middle of your TV tube, the pig balloons out, eventually to the point of a full-blown hog.)

Truecredit.com had yet another money-driven commercial airing at the same time. No voices were used. Just words dancing across the screen.

When your credit's good, your life is good.
Manage your credit. Manage your life. It's that simple.

Problem is, it isn't simple. It's because of those reasons exactly — credit, money, life — that people struggle.

Chapter 4

Bashing business

"I don't think corporate America knows what it's doing.
When there is no coercion, there is no such thing as losers."
— Aubie Baltin, retired CFA, CTA, CFP
January 2007

E ver owned a product that didn't work or stopped working before you thought it should? Ever pay for a service that you didn't get what was promised to you? Ever feel like you've been forced into doing something by a business or corporation.

Being forced to do something is called coercion.

When you think back to those instances, how long did it take to get them resolved? Was it fast enough for you? Did it drag on way too long? Did the company, corporation or small business you were dealing with actually resolve the issue or are you still left feeling empty-handed?

And what was the company's response as to why you weren't going to get what you wanted fixed or what were the consequences they were giving you? Did their rationale have to do with money, by chance?

That's the problem with business. It's all about money. At the customer's expense. A lot of times even when the service and products don't fulfill their promises, it boils down to an expense on your part in order to get the matter resolved. Not always, but a lot of times.

Need an example?

Ever bought a cordless phone and it went bad a long time before it should have or even within a warranty period? Maybe it was the battery that was the problem. That's easy, you figure. Just go to the store and pick up a new one. When you get to the store, you probably discovered the cost of the battery was nearly the cost of the phone itself, or more. Or maybe you couldn't even find the battery needed for that phone.

Time to buy another phone.

Forget you Sony. Nix that GE. Think again Motorola.

All told, it ended up being more

How much did they initially tell you you were going to pay? How much did you end up paying?

Surely, you've crossed paths with those questions at some point. Those scenarios are out there. All the time.

People are constantly being told one thing by one person and something different by another. What businesses have grown accustomed to telling customers is, "Well, I can't speak for what So and So told you earlier, but this is what you're being charged now." All told, of course, after your credit card has been charged. Or a bill has been sent out. Threats of collection agents in the works.

Case in point, T-Mobile, a cellular phone company, once told a customer he had the option of terminating his two-line phone service, but the female customer service representative handling the call didn't completely disclose any financial repercussions. Weeks later, that customer received a bill in excess of over $500 when all payments up to that time had been paid. And the customer didn't even use the service for a full month during that specific billing cycle. Under normal circumstances, his bill would've been $69, plus taxes.

T-Mobile assessed the customer with not one, but two early termination fees of $200 apiece. None of the fee amounts, let alone the number of fees, were ever disclosed to the customer in the initial conversation with the female call center representative. True, it may have been a classic example of laziness, a personal battle or some animosity that developed between the customer and T-Mobile's customer service agent, but a failure to communicate this to customers is wrong on any company or corporation's part. Let alone, a communications company such as

T-Mobile, which prides itself in excellent customer service and communicating skills on a people-wide basis.

T-Mobile later was sued in 2009 regarding early termination fees. The settlement offered customers who were burdened with ETFs a compensation package based on the amount of money T-Mobile coaxed out of customers who paid such. All of which was ruled by the United States District Court of New Jersey as a civil infringement on the phone company's customers.

T-Mobile also, for the longest time, operated under a seek-money first policy in regards to text messaging. Customers not wanting text messaging as an option, don't care to send text messages out or even receive them, but have service with T-Mobile, were unfortunately out of luck. If a text message popped up in that person's inbox on their phone, whether they open it or not, T-Mobile assessed a charge.

"It's part of the system," said Roberta, a T-Mobile customer service representative. "It's been that way, and will stay that way until someone else changes it."

Roberta had a last name. Most people do. She elected not to give it out. Not because of company policy. Because she chose not to.

"I can, and I don't want to," Roberta said in a terse manner on a late January 2007 day.

T-Mobile has a policy regarding media requests to call a designated number. The message states the line is to be used strictly by journalists.

A reporter called that number in the fall of 2006 and left a detailed message, stating requests to speak with T-Mobile CEO Robert Dotson.

Nobody from T-Mobile, let alone Robert Dotson, ever returned that reporter's call.

Sounds like a failure to communicate. A failure to communicate on a communication company's end. Isn't it nice how a communications company can choose not to communicate? Or simply doesn't know how to?

Courtesy or curt is the way in the corporate industry

Let's get the record straight, nowadays larger businesses, especially service-oriented corporations that operate primarily over the phone, are giving their employees way too much leeway in the types of responses they can say to customers. Yet, one false move, one bad word out of the customer's mouth and it's taboo.

We're talking the ultimate No-No.

"I'm going to release this call."

Click.

Businesses allow their representatives the ability to tell customers such things as, "Well, I'm not Verizon," or "I'm not Best Buy," or "You didn't talk to me before, I just get a paycheck from The Home Depot." Such responses are simple searches for technicalities. Loopholes. Ways to pin blame on the customer. Instead of just accepting the fact that when a customer refers to "them" or "you," and meaning the company as a whole, some employees get snooty.

Not to mention downright snotty.

"You told me I only had to pay this," a customer might say.

The employee's rejoinder: "Who's you? Ma'am, I haven't talked to you before."

"OK, well your company said I wouldn't have to pay this because it was being taken care of."

"I really apologize for the inconvenience, but I wasn't the person you spoke with before. I'm not privy to that conversation. This is your only option."

Essentially, it becomes a ploy to suspend the goal at hand and merely frustrate the customer. Either before or after they try to coax more money out of the individual who decided to do business with that company.

Bigger businesses will do anything to avoid accepting responsibility for problems that have caused friction with *their customers* in many cases. Especially if they are going to get more money out of the deal. Businesses tell customers one thing and then do another. They make promises to the customers, but then find ways to avoid fulfilling those promises when another employee steps in or fields a second, third or fourth call. Even worse, companies are notorious for requiring the individual to service themselves.

It happens all the time in the business of acquiring flight miles or credits with airlines hotel and car rental partners. Neither the airline nor the partner wants to assume responsibility for honoring the promises laid forth in the promotions *they* set up.

At least not without a fight.

Choice words

An Allentown, Penn., Quality Inn Hotel supervisor once told a customer if he stayed two nights at the hotel the customer and his girlfriend would each be awarded airline credits through a Southwest Airlines Rapid Rewards frequent flyer incentive program. The customer was willing to book two separate reservations, one for himself, the other for his chick. Two membership numbers were provided at the time of check-in. One for the guy, the other for his gal. The customer asked the hotel front desk clerk whether he needed two separate credit cards in order to fulfill the dual-credit airline promotion. Quality Inn's staff member and manager insisted that wasn't necessary.

Over a month later, the timeframe when credits are *supposed* to appear in any Rapid Rewards member's account, neither the guy nor girl had been awarded any airline credits. The customer contacted Southwest Airlines corporate offices in Dallas about the matter. Southwest Airlines' stance was the customer had to take it up with the hotel or the hotel chain. Quality Inn is a member of Choice

Hotels. Choice Hotels' main offices in Colorado told the customer it was up to the hotel itself to issue the credit.

You can see where this is going.

Run-around central.

That same day, the customer, benefitted by the proximity of his residence to the hotel, decided to go back to the hotel in person, receipt in his possession. His plan was to speak to the manager face-to-bace about the matter and attempt to gain both credits, one for the guy and another for the girl, as promised before any money changed hands on the night of the initial hotel stay. When the customer arrived at the hotel, the manager wasn't around. The front desk clerk who checked the guest in at the original time of arrival was working, however, but said he couldn't resolve the matter. He gave the customer the option of waiting for his supervisor to return. The customer elected to do so.

When the hotel manager of Middle Eastern descent finally returned, the customer started explaining the situation again. The manager simply didn't want to listen. He didn't want to accept responsibility for what he promised the customer, and it became a battle between the two.

The manager asked the customer for his receipt. When the customer gave it to him, the manager **ripped it up and dropped the torn pieces in the garbage**. The customer was furious at that point.

"Give that back to me," he demanded, standing on the other side of the check-in counter.

The manager didn't budge.

"Give that back to me."

Eventually, the manager pulled the receipt's pieces out of the garbage and handed them to the customer.

More words were exchanged.

"Get the f--- out of here," the manager screamed. "Get the f--- out of my hotel ... Do you understand what f--- means?"

The customer eventually walked out extremely unhappy, shouting back at the manager, still dissatisfied he and his girl didn't get what was promised to them in terms of the airlines credits.

When the customer called Choice Hotels' corporate office again later that day and explained what transpired at the hotel, Choice Hotels' supervisor staff's response was, "We're sorry that he would say that word to you. We're sorry that he ripped up your receipt." Choice Hotels supervisor staff eventually became annoyed that the customer made repeated references to the wording the manager told the man to his face.

But nothing got done to rectify the airlines credit situation. It was a lot of wasted time on the guy's part. Yet that time spent trying to resolve the issue with the hotel in person was the advice Choice Hotels' supervisor staff suggested the customer take to rectify the situation.

To no avail.

As for the whole swearing and cursing part of the equation, that's another story. It's a double standard.

When a customer uses foul language, raises his or her voice, employees tell them, "I don't have to listen to that. I'm going to release this call."

Click.

The customer is to blame. Regardless whether the problem at hand is the business' fault or not. Pay the bill and shut up.

Yet when a manager curses at a person— face to face, mind you— apparently it's acceptable. Acceptable to tell a customer whatever they feel, and still take their money in the process.

Comfort Suites home ... hardly

In December of 2006, a couple spent a night at a Baltimore/Washington International Airport Comfort Suites hotel in Linthicum, Md. The couple agreed to pay $89 for the room that night. After it was all said and done, the hotel charged the man's card an additional $74.40.

Oh, there was that "In room Safe" charge of a $1. *An In room Safe that was never used.*

Whatever.

There was that "state tax" of $4.45. Tack on another "occupancy tax" of $6.23. That brought the room charges to $100.68. It ran on a credit card belonging to the man.

The man signed for the room charge upon check-in. The couple checked out after one night's stay.

Three days later, the man's card was hit with another "room charge" of $56. Then came a $2.80 "state tax" and a $3.92 "occupancy tax." All told, an additional $62.72.

The hotel billed the customer for "room charges." Terry L. Hammel, Comfort Suites BWI front office manager, claimed in a written document the charges totalling $62.72 were for "parking charges."

How a person can park in a room is beyond imagination.

The man, nor the woman, ever signed anything with regards to authorizing parking charges. Yet Hammel's staff charged the man's card anyway.

Without authorization.

"We feel that's not unreasonable charges to be charging," said Dave, a BWI Comfort Suites front desk personnel member.

Hammel stated the following in a written document trying to justify the additional charges:

I know that you have asked for written documentation for your extended parking. Given the circumstances of not being informed in advance, of course it is unavailable.

Comfort Suites kept the money. Hammel later told the man, "You do what you've gotta do."

You're probably wondering whether the man or the woman ever had plans to stay at that hotel again, aren't you?

Know their name? It's still our game

Sometimes, in order to get resolution, businesses ask customers what the names of each and every person they spoke to in prior business-related conversations. But service-oriented companies many times advise their employees not to provide first and last names.

Yet you'll need to know who that customer service rep, technical support specialist, supervisor or management staff member's name was to move forward with your problem the next time you talk to someone from that company. Just so you have it ready to verify what *they*, as a company, elect to put in the notes on your account.

If they even took the time to do their jobs and actually put something in the notes.

And the next day or two when you call back because the company hasn't resolved the issue, done what they, meaning the employees you spoke with, said they were going to do, or someone from that company hasn't returned a call when one employee promised you would receive follow-up correspondence, you're left stranded.

A female associate from T-Mobile once assured a customer she would call back one day after speaking with him late at night to resolve an issue she said she generally didn't want to get overlooked. She claimed she couldn't talk any longer that night because T-Mobile's communication's system wouldn't allow her to proceed, but that she promised to call back the next day.

She never made good on her promise.

You're probably guessing what happened. The next time the customer called back, the customer got someone different on the phone.

It was time to start explaining again.

It's a never-ending cycle that takes way too much time to resolve nowadays. Whenever there's a conflict regarding a business matter and the calls get interrupted, technically dislodged or abruptly ended because either party hangs up after starting to address the issue, but neither side gets anywhere, it turns into a recurring cycle.

The customer has to start all over again, including verifying she or he is who they say they are. Everyone knows how long of a process just identifying yourself can be these days.

It's extremely frustrating to the customers, especially when the matter involves money.

Frankly, businesses know that. They know the system they have in place. They also know eventually it will discourage some customers, scare others with flat-out threats over looming collection agency-induced actions, and simply frustrate the heck out of people to the point they'll just eat the costs and pay for something they feel strongly they're not responsible for. Just to let the headache go.

That's wrong. A person shouldn't have to do that.

Especially considering a business' underlying message nowadays is, "our sole purpose is to make money."

At whatever costs necessary.

Even worse, when you, as a customer, financially can not pay bills because you simply don't have the funds because of factors out of your control, businesses often take a "We-Don't-Care" mentality and threaten to ruin your credit score, send you to collections or, even worse, add fees onto your bill. Especially if you don't pay on time.

Part of the problems facing why people can't and don't pay certain bills on time is because other businesses have tacked on late fees, surcharges, penalties and so on, which depletes that person's resources a little more.

Yet there's only so much money to go around.

Some people have it, many people don't.

"It's a tough thing," said Rich Mudd, a Los Angeles regional account manager for Boiron, a homeopathic company in the health industry. "Who you know, and are you in the right place at the right time. That's the real thing about money.

"People born into money are not worrying about what kind of playing field there is. There's more than enough money for everyone out there, but it's a matter of how we're going to get people access to it. We don't have pure capitalism. When we start to tweak it all the time, we run into problems."

Cash-crunched companies

Virginia Hill, a vitamin store owner who ran a successful business in a nearly dilapidated part of Miami, eventually moved with her husband to shack up with family in Tennessee. She sold her store in Miami, one where her knowledge of the industry allowed her to pay bills and live a good life in South Beach. Sunshine wasn't ever much of a concern.

But her husband Gene eventually thought it would be better to bank the rest of their years in the hills of a more serene Tennessee environment. He carried on with his physical labor line of work, running a family business out of their barn and the family's extended land offerings. Their home was big enough to house three families, and they followed the Lord in their daily lives.

Virginia also owned a vitamin store in Jefferson City, Tenn., a nutrition outlet that didn't receive nearly as much traffic as her location in a sketchy part of Miami. For a while, her daughter, Debbie, ran the Tennessee store. Eventually Hill and her grand daughter, Shannon, took over control of the store. Ginny often moaned about the need to attract more customers into the store. For a while, she never found much time to get into her business herself because she invested more of her time handling the administrative, customer service and bookkeeping duties of her husband's trade while he handled the blue collar work in the barn with their son, Ronnie.

Ginny also played the role of mother to her grandchildren, constantly prodding them about the right way to live. Her husband often went through daily scripture readings with the family to raise awareness to other parts of their life they deemed most important. After firsthand experiences with practicing ministers, they helped oversee deliverance sessions to drive evil spirits and demons away from people beset with constant baggage and recurring negative issues. They received professional instruction from local ministers who trained at the University of Tennessee about 45 minutes away in Knoxville.

Still, even a woman trying to do the right thing, even a business owner who was successful, knowledgeable and professional at her craft and sure of herself as a Christian, had constraints. Ginny wasn't shy in proclaiming her credit card bills climbed to $20,000. Being a successful business owner didn't allow her to erase that debt with the snap of a finger. She just made monthly payments.

"It would be great if it were a free society," Ginny said as 2007 neared the completion of its second full week. "I would say the last three years it's been stressful."

She had an accountant analyze her books, which told her what the numbers would allow her to do. But she didn't relish it, not even with someone else doing the math for her. After all, she was constantly crunching numbers for her husband.

"This is like someone that has high blood pressure," Ginny said. "There's too much stress involved in running your own business."

Other business owners have felt the same way.

Car business culpability

Goodpaster left a high-paying sales industry job to eventually find his way into teaching. After moving his family on three major occasions, Goodpaster wanted out of the sales industry, a line of work he noticed was going south quickly. He was selling textiles to the automotive industry, but wanted out because of the practices going on and the turns the industry were taking.

"A million dollars today doesn't go as far," Goodpaster said. "It's great that we have a lot more millionaires, but it doesn't mean as much."

Goodpaster left the sales industry with distaste. Distaste for factors not in his control.

While selling textiles to the automotive industry, he noticed some of the unfair practices in business. He knew firsthand what was going on because of the crooked gamesmanship in the automotive industry. It had indirect and direct effects on him. Goodpaster claims Ford, GM and Chrysler were forcing their suppliers to provide a minimum of 5-10 percent price reductions on a yearly basis. If the suppliers, which Goodpaster's company happened to be one of, failed to comply with the automakers' demands, the suppliers would be penalized eventually.

"Whether you gave it to them or not they took it," Goodpaster said. "It's an unauthorized deduction on an invoice. The only thing they were really dealing with is cash.

"If you didn't give it to them and you shipped your products to them in that calendar year, the invoices would be reflected on their actions. Every year they were asking for a 5% percent getback."

And if you didn't comply with the Big Three, you weren't playing by "the rules."

A man who worked for Ford and eventually took a buyout from one of its Michigan plants before moving across the country, reaffirmed Goodpaster's thoughts. He couldn't do anything but nod "yes" and say "uh huh" to Goodpaster's claims.

The North American Free Trade Agreement opened up the doors to allow foreign countries to gain a share of the market.

"All these companies went bankrupt because of automotive," Goodpaster said. "Ford put 'em out of business. Ford was one of the toughest that I dealt with."

So companies went under, people lost jobs, people couldn't pay their bills, tempers flared, companies flexed their muscles and, in the end, foreign companies got paid.

"We can't make enough in the U.S. because we keep farming it out to other countries," Goodpaster said. "How is it free and equitable for the U.S.? Nobody's buying our stuff. Ross Perot said it would happen, and it has. That's the biggest fault that we have done. We've got to be competitive.

"What automotive did by opening up NAFTA, it caused them to stop cutting wages. It's the ultimate payback. Their greed is what got 'em."

Goodpaster left automotive sales, figuring he'd never make millions as a teacher. He felt a sense of security in the need for his secondary career choice. But he pointed out that schools draw much of their funds from taxpayers. Even as a teacher, he had reservations about the future and his role in it upon switching professions. He held those concerns because the red flags stemming from economic conditions that signaled great potential for major unemployment. Without jobs, who would pay the taxes that fund the schools? Then, in turn, who's going to pay the teachers?

A lack of jobs equals a lack of money.

At least that's what the world we live in now suggests. Unless the government and people in power want to pay for everything.

"We are working ourselves into a corner," Goodpaster said.

Woe are the money seekers. Ross Perot save us.

Happy house hunting

So you enjoy the idea of paying to live. Great. So you decide to buy a new house. Great. You seek out a new development and start the process. It should be exciting.

Deb Vannatta, a sales associate for K Hovnanian, a home builder, thinks so anyway.

"This should be a fun time," Vannatta said.

Many times it's not fun. Not when you consider the whole process required, the way mortgage companies and lenders judge people based on that score at the end of their name and the procedures they require of you. On top of that, homebuilders and their loan partners want you to do the work for yourself. They want you to fill out information on-line. They want you to provide tax documents, pay stubs, etc. Essentially, they want you to service *them* so *you* can buy a home.

K Hovnanian, a home builder that sells houses in multiple states, bases its headquarters out of Red Bank, N.J. Its company-umbrellaed loan offices reside in Florida, or at least some of their loan specialists anyway. K Hovnanian encourages home seekers to use their loan department. But K Hovnanian's loan department doesn't always want to honor other companies loan products that are available, even though they suggest they'll let you use whomever you want to get the best price for your home.

In 2007, K Hovnanian came across an instance where home seekers presented a loan product that eliminated mortgage insurance premium costs by structuring the loan into separate bridge loans. K Hovnanian gives customers the option to use their outside lenders if they don't want to use K Hovnanian's loan specialists. But they insist the home seekers must pay an additional 5 percent in upfront costs.

One K Hovnanian loan officer called a customer after running credit reports. He told the customers both of their credits were excellent. He eventually worked up a good faith estimate based on the information provided to him by the customer. The good faith estimate stated a higher figure for the monthly house payments than originally estimated and provided to the customers on an in-house visit to one of the K Hovnanian sales communities.

It was roughly $200 more.

The couple didn't like the sounds of that. They asked the home developer sales associate and loan officer to seek other options to restructure the loan in an effort to find a lower payment. K Hovnanian elected not to work up another estimate.

"I'm sure he did the best he could," the sales associate told the home seeker, referring to the loan officer's efforts.

"No he didn't," one of the home seekers responded. "He was lazy. He only worked up one quote. There are other programs out there. Is it a matter of being educated? I can put you in contact with another mortgage specialist who offers these programs, and quoted me a better rate."

Prior to all this, the customers agreed not to bring another real estate agent into the equation, a move that would allow K Hovnanian to retain thousands of more dollars. K Hovnanian's sales associate told the couple they could bring in another real estate agent if they wanted. She also told them they were happy to pay another real estate agent who represented them. But her comments were made after the good faith estimate was laid out, and it was made clear to the customer K Hovnanian's stance was against working up another quote by restructuring the loan a different way. What K Hovnanian probably should have said was that it didn't feel like going to any more trouble to sell the house to the couple.

More like, "Take it or leave it."

The couple walked away from the deal.

"Sorry we couldn't do business," the sales associate said.

On Aug. 2, 2010, *USA Today* ran a page 1A story headlined, "Skid seen in rate of owning homes: Foreclosures push fall toward '60 low."

The lead of the story said it all.

Millions of houses on the verge of foreclosure threaten to send homeownership to its lowest level in 50 years, according to new industry estimates.

You get the feeling K Hovnanian is rethinking the way they do business, and its inability to try to accomodate potential buyers.

On the same day the doom of foreclosure story ran in The Nation's Newspaper with the blue and white world wide globe logo at the top of the front page, another story ran headlined, "Low yields deflate money funds." It was centered at the top Section B, categorized Money.

Its first two paragraphs read:

Money fund assets have fallen by $1.1 trillion since January 2009, leading to two questions: Where did it go? And why hasn't more left.

The exodus from money market mutual funds isn't surprising. The average money fund yields 0.04%, according to iMoneyNet, which tracks the funds. At that rate, a $10,000 investment in the average fund will return just $4 in a year. A quarter of the nation's 1,643 funds — 415 — yield zero, iMoneyNet says.

A scary thought to say the least what's happening to your money. Who's doing what with it once you "put it away for safekeeping?" And who can guarantee it'll be around when you go to cash in on it?

A Citimortgage account supervisor located in Montana suggested to a customer calling in to make a payment on his condominium that there was no real reason to discuss issues on a grand scale concerning money. Her rationale:

"It's all corporate now."

Exactly, and people like this Montana Citimortgage employee are getting taken advantage of because of the "corporate cornering the market" concept. Oh so, just let corporations get away with whatever they want.

Nothing like a little greed to push people around.

"We shouldn't be letting the businesses run us," Goodpaster said.

Goodpaster's home is not far from downtown Nashville. He chose a quiet community with nice homes to make his long-term residence.

On one side of the street he lives on, water companies were charging homeowners roughly $30 monthly standards and drawing their water supply from one source. On the other side of the street, the water supplier was charging $70 and drawing their water supply from another source. But the residents on the one side of the street aren't privileged to the water supply of those on the other side.

"Laws," said Goodpaster, a man beat up by the thought of the bills' discrepancy, frustrated, yet genuine sarcasm in his voice.

"Laws prevent you from doing it. I could run a pipe myself. That's a lot of money when you think about it."

Forty dollars a month more. Four hundred and eighty dollars a year more. It's a lot of money that affects many homeowners. Which, by the way, translates to many people. Yet companies are getting away with it, and the decision makers behind those companies are benefitting the most.

"When is enough enough?" Goodpaster vented. "CEOs should not be making 23 million a year just in bonuses. I think these guys are out of touch.

"What figure can people justify for how much money a CEO makes? The Commander in Chief of our country makes what $250 to $500 thousand and CEOs are making $23 million in bonuses.

"Wow."

The President of the United States' original salary was $25,000 in 1789. That's when George Washington took his oath of office as the first president of the United States on April 30, 1789 on the balcony of Federal Hall on Wall Street in New York. In 1873, the president's pay was doubled to $50,000. In 1907, Congress approved an additional $25,000 annual stipend for office-related expenses. By 1969, the president's earnings increased to $200,000 with an additional $100,000 for travel and $50,000 for expenses. In 2001, the salary doubled again to $400,000, with $50,000 in expense write-offs. Because the president's "duties" lifestyle incurs more expenses than the $50,000 limit, federal government agencies often take on the presidential "extras."

The history of the U.S. president's escalating pay suggests greed in itself. Especially considering the president is the person ultimately responsible for assuring a better life for all citizens. But not all citizens are surviving financially. And many never get raises. Not even 25 cent raises, let alone $25,000 or $250,000 raises like *some* people.

All told, Goodpaster is right. CEOs are getting away with way too much. (See earlier references to erstwhile Home Depot chief Bob Nardelli and his $210 million severance package in 2007.)

Corporate corruption

When people make big money, people talk a big game.

"Corporations were never intended to be equal with citizens, and today they are out of hand," a former Chicago Bulls insider who eventually sought out the vitamin business as a career when he became concerned with personal health issues.

"Capitalism is a flawed system. It's not always a fair system. It's a worldwide issue that's been going on for thousands and thousands of years. They don't plant the seed in front of you. You have to find it yourself. It's a very complicated process. Unfortunately it's true. It's a real serious problem.

"It's utter nonsense what's occurring within the trade force. There's something disproportionate about how a CEO of a company gets millions of dollars for walking away from a position. It's slavery. We have not set up a system that is equitable. It's sort of a rigged system."

Oh really?

"Money changes certain people," said the former professional basketball insider who shared a close friendship with a financial genius who studied the currency system since he worked the floors of the New York stock market.

"In general, people just want to make enough money to survive. The rich people get a lot of breaks. You've got a few greedy, powerful people who control everything. I'm convinced people that are in a position of power, they don't know what they're doing. They don't have a blueprint. I think its days are coming to an end as we know them. When we do things purely for self, we've missed the boat."

It's quite obvious corporations have their own rules. Rules that they set up, that don't matter what type of rights people have. Or rights that were set up long ago that seemingly nobody adheres to much any more. Corporations like to claim they are "private" now, so they can do as they please. So they can set up their own rules.

Is the country where corporations reside considered private? Is the locality the businesses operate out of considered private?

Why don't the corporations just deal with private people then? Are there any people out there that are private, excluded from the rest of society? Maybe corporations should just do business with those individuals. These companies also have a non-communication clause, of course.

"Our CEO doesn't have a number," comes the most-commonly used response.

Uh huh. Dude makes $23 million a year in extras, but doesn't have enough money to get a phone.

Yeah ...

"Well, we can't give out our CEO's number," is another typical response.

"We don't have access to that information."

Funny how a company can have all that money, but never figures out a way to provide resources to locate a phone number. Or find a way to communicate with people who do have it. So do these CEOs really exist or are they just pseudo personas?

The fact of the matter is the employees themselves can't even communicate with headquarters in most occasions. They can't even verify policies with the company they work for. They can't even talk to fellow "employees" elevated to a different status in the company they work for.

"I worked in the corporate world outside of where I'm working now, and I never had any way of getting in touch with my corporate manager," said Julie Farrell, who after switching jobs from one corporate office to another, found herself in Springfield, Mo.

Naturally.

This business of sports

Late in 2006, the New York Yankees were hit with a $26 million luxury tax for being high-priced spenders in this game of acquiring the big names in baseball. The penalty raised the team's taxes, set by Major League Baseball's league offices, of course, to $97.75 million over a four-year span, dating back to 2002.

"We've become numb to the dollar amounts," said ESPN SportsCenter anchor John Anderson.

Anderson moved from place to place in his career. His parents both grew up on farms that had been passed down in a family lineage method of sharing. A noble concept indeed. He was raised on a farm in Wisconsin. One of those farms was later altered, for lack of better terms or political correctness, because the government decided transportation was important.

"Now there was a highway cutting through it," Anderson explained. "It just made me sick to my stomach."

That idea of industrialization became the norm in the United States. See land, build something there. See a desert, lay down some mortar. Begin construction.

All for one main purpose.

To make money.

It's the American way. It's society's way.

Forget the idea that God-given land had any intrinsic value. Dismiss this idea of aesthetic beauty. Land's beauty has offerings of its own. If there's free land, there's opportunities to make money. Maybe, in America, we can thank Christopher Columbus for it. Whoever deserves the credit, thanks.

Too bad you're not around today to benefit.

But honestly, who really gave man the authority to put price tags on land and determine how much they could get away with?

Anyway, Anderson lived in Tulsa, Okla., and Phoenix, Ariz., doing TV work after his graduation from Missouri. He came out of college, attending what he referred to as "one of the best J schools," (journalism schools for the loose-term uninformed) struggling to find a job that paid him the equivalent of what he said he could have made at McDonald's. Boy, was his mom happy about that. Nonetheless, his career and travels took him places. On an early January day in 2007, he was driving around the rolling hills of Connecticut when his eyes gazed upon some of the upper Northeast's living conditions. He remembered thinking about some of those homes months earlier.

"My God, this was the people's summer homes that they lived in for *eight weeks*," Anderson resonated.

His thoughts obviously made people who never made their way up to Connecticut realize something, something that Anderson himself had on his mind those days.

This idea of money.

"Which, by the way, there is some money in this state," Anderson pointed out in his natural, cynical tone.

And let's not lie, money changes people.

"It's a devil's advocate sometimes," Anderson said. "It is kooky. It's expensive to do *anything*."

Including falling in love. But you don't need to tell Anderson about that.

"I know. I have a daughter who's three," Anderson began. "She just looks at you when she sees a car and says she wants one. I have to go out the next day and try to find a way to finance it."

He was kidding. But you get the point.

Weddings aren't cheap either. Even the paperwork just to "ratify" a marital relationship at city or county offices costs money.

As a sports highlight anchor, Anderson has witnessed the growing greed and money in sports. He's had to provide commentary on sports news stories and even action highlights that reference cash.

Cash calls, you might say.

"You put it in because it has some relevance," Anderson reasoned.

Either that, or one's mind is strictly focusing on the money.

On camera when providing the lead-in for a Milwaukee Bucks-New Jersey Nets game highlight Dec. 13, 2006, Anderson had these words, "I think we all enjoy big bucks. Let's not lie about that." A few weeks later, after the Christmas holidays, but still in the midst of bowl game blitz and season-ending pro football news on Jan. 4, 2007, when discussing the resignation of Pittsburgh

Steelers coach Bill Cowher, Anderson made the comment, "Boy, you hate to be without a paycheck when you got a three million dollar mortgage out there."

Wonder how mortgage companies reacted to that?

On Jan. 31 that same year, while doing a show with fellow SportsCenter anchor Scott Van Pelt, Anderson had these comments:

"I love big bucks, and I make no bones about it."

When talking about how the University of Alabama lured Nick Saban away from the Miami Dolphins to coach football, Anderson sorted out all the rationale the school used in claiming what its motives were for bringing in a coach who still had years left on a contract in the professional game. Saban's contract became the richest contract in all of college football, and the money was all guaranteed. Saban's contract was an eight-year deal worth $32 million, plus $700-800 thousand in bowl game bonuses. He had three years left on his deal with the Dolphins.

ESPN's Chris Mortensen reported at a meeting in Saban's house with his wife and Dolphins owner Wayne Huizenga, that Saban told the business owner magnet-slash-football team owner:

"If you really want me to stay, I'll stay."

Huizenga's response: "No, you have to follow your heart. You have my blessing."

Later that day, Saban landed on a private flight in Alabama, ready to shake hands with the Crimson Tide.

The University of Alabama had their own explanations why Saban was brought to Tuscaloosa, their own spin on it all. Anderson had one of his own.

"No, you just bought a football coach because you want to win games," Anderson said.

"Guys chase paychecks more than they used to. At some point, it becomes the barometer."

Sometimes sports personalities and ... uh ... people chase paychecks, too. It's called living the American Dream.

It's called greed.

Anderson was a Green Bay Packers season ticket holder. When the team decided it wanted to make improvements to Lambeau Field, he grieved over the idea season ticket holders were hit with seat license fees.

"There's no kid's section," Anderson bemoaned. "Right now the guy in Brown County is getting hit with a tax. Who cares if you raised the rates. Pretty soon you got to make a decision."

He spoke of a woman, who, in published reports, proclaimed her allegiance to the Packers. She had season tickets. In Green Bay, there isn't much life outside of the Packers. It takes a while to migrate to Milwaukee, so those in and around Lambeau know football weekends are all about the Green and Yellow. Days which by the way, bring in the green. Nonetheless, this woman was diehard. But she was running short on money. She didn't want to give up her seats, so she elected not to pay her heat bill in order to keep her seats. After all, once those seats are gone, someone else scoops them up and professional organizations don't hold any loyalties to their fans. They just want the money.

"In sports, the money is outrageous," Anderson said.

Outrageous even in his trade.

Anderson signed a contract with ESPN, but he confessed his agreement didn't bank the largest deal in the broadcaster's chair.

"That's why Chris Berman and Dan Patrick are legends," he said.

Home sweet home, hah

Home builders claim they really don't make much money off building houses. Maybe because they're shredding up the little guys. Little guys they hire to do contract work.

Centex Homes was accused of forcing its contractors to perform work without paying for it. In essence, Centex tried to secure as much free labor as possible. As a reward, the home developer offered contractors "A-B-C-D" awards to contractors who "played by the rules." Or Centex used free t-shirt or gift gimmicks to contractors who bought into the low-balling business.

If Centex ever found a problem with the work its contractors performed, it would remit payments lower than the terms laid forth in the contracts.

Centex once failed to fully pay a dumpster removal service servicing its Rolling Ridge housing community in Howell, Mich., the full amount of the parties' agreement. The dumpster service fired back by littering Rolling Ridge's streets with the garbage materials, lined up in a sea of piles as high as the dumpsters themselves.

Other developers were tagged with similar labels. Pulte Homes was blamed for unfair practices of their own. Still, other developers were accused of underpricing bidders to the point it cost the contractors money to do the work.

Some contractors eventually went out of business.

Sounds like the automotive industry revisted.

Chiming in with churches

Even churches and the "business" known as ministry are beset by financial deficiencies. Radio ministries are in constant search of money to remain on the air. Non-profit ministries even. Churches themselves, regardless of whether one person walks through the doors or 1,000, require money to pay bills. An electric bill is an electric bill, no matter if it's in a temple or a home.

To illustrate the church's calls for monetary support, here is a letter that circulated in December of 2006 by a radio ministry program called, "In Season and Out of Season," based out of East Boston, Mass.:

Dear Child of God,

It is beginning to look a lot like snowmen, icicles, etc. The Grinch has stolen Christ from Christmas in most places. We live in a pagan society, and Jesus is hated and not even tolerated by the populace. The Word of God is getting more difficult to hear. Amos tells us that there would be a famine, not of bread and water, but of the Word of God. The Cross is barely proclaimed and people have become immune to Jesus.

It is time to read the signs of the times. Every religion is tolerated, save those who worship the God of Israel. It is exciting as well as challenging during these times to proclaim the Lord Jesus. MANY have asked me where I get the energy to proclaim Jesus. It is easy to proclaim the One you Love even when you are living in deep arid times.

Only the Word of God and the Eucharist empowered by the Holy Spirit will change things. We are beyond techniques and gimmicks. Real faith that will offer its life to the Savior is the only answer.

Sometimes I feel like John the Baptist in jail ... "Is it all worth it, why do I continue?" And then the Lord sends me a letter from a prisoner telling me that the broadcasts have literally saved his life. The proclamation of the Holy Word of God is the number one vocation of the Church; I want to reach the world one at a time, and you are the ones who give me this opportunity through your prayers and gifts. Please set aside three minutes a day and pray for me, that I fulfill the destiny that the Lord Jesus calls me to do.

I will celebrate Holy Mass for you and your loved ones on Christmas. Know I depend on your gifts to continue this most important work.

In Jesus' Love,
Fr. Tom+

Just thought I'd let you know

In the fall of 2006, AT&T told a customer he would secure a phone service for a designated amount. It was under the assumption that if a customer agreed to pay that amount to a company, or in this case, "corporation," the company, AT&T by name, would agree to provide the type of service the customer was entitled to.

Let's just put it this way, repeated service requests were made. And nothing was ever done.

A letter was then sent to AT&T's CEO at the time. The head honcho. Guy in charge of that corporation, or at least the guy AT&T claimed was in charge, Ed Whittaker.

Here's the letter, minus some personal information digits — "for security purposes," just to mock the most-often used phrase used these days:

12-22-06

AT&T
Ed Whittaker
P.O. Box 580
Lee Summit, MO 64063

Ed:

Your company has severely angered me, in addition to failing to provide the type of service it promised.

First, I was assured AT&T would send a technician out to my apartment to have another jack installed within my apartment if I agreed to pay for installation charges when I initially contacted AT&T in the fall to activate phone service at my Pennsylvania residence. AT&T dropped the ball, and did not do what it, as a company, said it would.

Second, while AT&T had ownership of my phone number (XXX-XX-XXXX) — it no longer owns this number — I could not receive incoming phone calls. A call, initiated on my part, using another phone service provider's technology, was made to AT&T. I spoke with a Jason in Kansas City regarding this issue. On Nov. 8, 2006, I also spoke to an Anna, who while providing the confirmation number W7201108, told me verbatim, "Right now you just have to disregard that bill since we are still making corrections." Anna's statement was made regarding a bill that was extremely overpriced, and with obvious greedy intentions on AT&T's part, trying to coerce me to pay for service that did not fully comply with the promises and guarantees AT&T makes to its customers or at least to me personally. Read above for illustrations of what sort of problems AT&T has caused me. Read the next paragraph for another illustration of AT&T's poor service.

On Dec. 8, 2006, I spoke with a female who gave me the name of Toni, telling me she was located in Los Angeles. Nothing was accomplished that night other than a waste of time. The phone conversation was disrupted at 7 p.m. EST. Upon calling back, I could not get through to anyone at AT&T because of your company's policy to limit calls up until 7 p.m., at least during the week, from the calling area the customer is located in. When I spoke to Sue on Dec. 19, 2006, she told me AT&T didn't even have AT&T employees in Los Angeles. Sue reiterated my suspicions, that I was lied to by whomever I was talking to on Dec. 8.

Bottom line, I am using all of this information -- facts, of course -- in a book I am writing. I have authored one book already. And I refuse to pay for a $103.09 bill AT&T is threatening me with, especially considering all of the above-stated facts have not only frustrated me, but essentially coaxed me into even having to take time to write this letter.

Just thought I'd let you know Ed.

Jim McCurdy
(XXX-XXX-XXXX)

Maybe there were no lies on Toni's part. Maybe there really was a Toni that worked for AT&T in Los Angeles. Maybe Sue didn't know there were AT&T locations in Los Angeles. But if that was the case, Sue shouldn't have stated otherwise. Or maybe AT&T and Ed Whittaker just need to train their employees better on the geographical locations of its company offices.

Either way, because of the stance and principles that this book is trying to make people realize, the author of that letter, the author of this book, called AT&T and finally, after the long waiting game, number-pressing rhetoric customers have to go through just to speak to people nowadays, let alone listen to an automated, once-recorded voice-over (ahh breathe, you're off the waiting game hook) the customer actually reached a physical voice. Following a long drawn-out process — just as AT&T strung the customer along and forced frustration — time and accented the battle for what was right to be put forth in writing, the customer told AT&T to take the money and run. A credit card was provided to the AT&T customer service employee to pay off the entire bill before AT&T or Ed Whittaker even cared to respond, and the customer essentially told AT&T to go bye-bye.

By the way, the customer entrusted his credit card numbers with a man named Ramon, who said he worked out of an AT&T Los Angeles location.

Just thought I'd let you know Ed. Your company got some money. And you either don't know how to read letters or don't care to respond. Let alone let all your employees know which cities you operate in.

Bad business busts down doors

Businesses have obviously ticked more than one person off. They've probably taken you to the cleaners once or twice. Did you ever do anything about it? Or did you let those corporations bully you around?

Some have elected to take matters into their own hands. Some have spoken publicly to the decision makers in charge. Some have written letters, the method most big companies try to encourage to avoid any in-person confrontations and simply avoid the issues. Others have went so far as creating companies that detail good and bad practices in business.

Better Business Bureau beware.

Chapter 5

Pocket-poking stories

"Money can lead to exploitation."
— A preacher in Phoenix, Ariz.
September 2007

People are affected by money nowadays in endless ways. And it's gotten way too nasty.

Why all the fuss about money?

"It's evil, and it's not good and everyone should just burn it," said Bernd Friedlander, a doctor from San Mateo, Calif. "It's the greed."

Damn right it's greed.

While arguing with a caller on his radio show "The Herd," ESPN air personality Colin Cowherd went off on a guy named Jeff.

"McDonald's didn't find out how to make a hamburger. They found out how to sell it," Cowherd said in his usual annoyingly overbearing tone. "ESPN, *SportsCenter* and ESPN Radio didn't create sports. They found out how to sell it.

"You want to make money, which creates a better life, find out something that people like to talk about."

Money doesn't always create a better life. Sometimes it causes problems. And sometimes people don't like to talk about it.

Selling out for superiority

Ron Jarvis, a successful salesperson in Minnesota, has watched his own bank account experience the ebb and flow of financial rifts. From high tide to low — at least in his terms — he's watched his days as a family man deteriorate, his character challenged in the workplace by an ex-wife and her father, mind you, and his credit score take hits because of the resulting long legal issues.

"If you don't think money can't buy happiness, you certainly don't shop at the right stores," Jarvis quipped, citing a phrase he heard ages earlier.

"No, I think money is one big giant pain in the ass. But I'm happy. I don't let money define me. It's one of the best things if you've got it, and it creates a lot of problems if you don't. It creates a lot of problems if you have it, too."

Jarvis endured two divorces before remarrying a third time. He's witnessed his marriages unravel before him, partly because of the money issue and partly because of unfaithful choices. Sometimes, having too much money can lead to unfaithful choices. (See professional athletes and entertainers.)

So was money an issue that contributed to the cause of divorce for Jarvis?

"Yeah, because they ended up having a lot of money," he said, his own conscience starting to nibble at him. "The bank of infidelity, when you make a deposit, is very, very brutal. It's very costly, emotionally and financially. So I've learned my lessons. I apologize to God for a lot of the things I did. I've grown up a lot. I went through a kick in the head for awhile."

Kick in the head because he lost funds to lawyers. He lost wives. His children were separated from him on a daily basis. His credit score took major hits, and maybe most significantly, he feels a sense of guilt. A sense of contributing to wrongdoing because he had the means and money to do so. To be persuasive and let money talk.

Students strapped for cash

It can be a scary, tempting, treacherous device indeed, this concept of money. It can have effects on the way we think, the choices we make, the fears we have and the anxiety caused by the pressure-filled world we live in. Bottom line, everyone, under the current society system we live in, is affected, influenced and tempted by money.

Even at ages you may not expect, let alone wish upon. We're talking adolescents or kids, whichever you prefer.

"Money is a stressful thing," said Alyssa Sharples, a 16-year-old waitress at Villa Venice in Great Meadows, N.J., during her junior year at Hackettstown High School in 2006-07.

A high school student who played basketball for the New Jersey school, situated in the hometown of the Snickers bar, Sharples is a sharp cookie. She carried an As and Bs report card. She's liked by friends, had a football player for a boyfriend during high school. But none of that changed the fact that money had resonating effects on her at a young age.

"I'm trying to save for a car," Sharples said, almost helpless at a seemingly insurmountable challenge.

That's why she was waitressing while playing sports and going to school.

Full time.

Fighting for fairness

Goodpaster held deep insights in the automotive industry as it relates to overseas capitalism. Goodpaster eventually became a teacher in Tennessee. He studied market trends, paid close attention to how money cursed his former line of work. He foresaw the world headed down a treacherous path.

He cited globalization of the economy and its effects on the automotive industry from the patterns he witnessed personally. He watched as companies he dealt with directly or indirectly were shut down based on some of the practices those companies followed.

Is the system fair? Are all people treated equal?

"Hell no," Goodpaster retorted without hesitation.

He's got a point.

"I know money can cause problems for people," said a Phoenix woman who won a share of a 2006 lottery.

Society sucks to some

Will, a money-troubled young adult who never graduated high school, moved from place to place in his adolescent and young 20s life. He lived in the Phoenix, Philadelphia and Delaware areas. He got himself into a bind on numerous occasions with the law, employers, financial institutions, family and landlords.

"I'm young and society pisses me off, and unknowingly I am revolting against society," Will said late in 2006. "I know one day I will be a millionaire so there is some comfort in that fact, but right now I'm pissed off at the world because life revolves around money. I think it's one day going to be a masterpiece, painted by Picasso."

His big bucks dream was a result of his parents share in winning an Arizona lottery in 2006.

Earlier that year, during a time of financial need, while Will held down a steady job as an auto parts salesman at a car dealership in Peoria, Ariz., he and another friend, who carried his own criminal record, elected to take some wheels and tires that were laying aside on the dealer's grounds. It was sort of an "off day," this sunny spring Saturday. The plan was Will's idea.

"I said, 'I got a great idea, let's steal wheels and tires and sell 'em,'" Will later confessed, replaying the incidents surrounding his doom days at the dealership.

He later found himself troubled by lawsuits. Early the next Monday morning, Will showed up for work, driven by his other friend and culprit in crime who already had a felony to his record in another state. Upon his arrival at work, police were waiting for him. The dealership's management called law enforcement officials after a gentleman the two misfits tried to sell the wheels and tires called the dealership, inquiring about the stolen goods. Will and his friend saw no harm because the parts were just sitting aside and no one was using them. The dealership didn't appear to be doing anything with them, nor did it offer hints it had use for the old car parts. Still, the wheels and tires belonged to the dealer, the dealership claims.

Will, who had previous run-ins with police for driving violations that caused other problems, had swapped residencies on the East Coast and in the sun's Southwest. He was, at times, with his natural mother out East.

Later that 2006 summer, Will elected to be responsible and show up for court in Glendale, Ariz., to address the stealing incident. A woman working at the court that day told him after his name was called and he appeared at the window that the case was dropped.

A relief. One burden off his plate.

He called his step mom the minute he walked out of the court, giving her the good news.

Later that fall, around the time the moving violations perpetuated to haunt him from his past, Will received a letter in the mail, explaining the case was reopened.

Knock, knock. Not over yet.

Will had problems just getting to work those days because of the traffic violations that limited and eventually caused full suspension of his license privileges. He soon lost his job, one at another car dealership that paid him more money than the one he was fired from, because he was constantly showing up late for work. The tardiness stemmed from his driving record's multiple violations that forced him to taxi or bus into work -- which cost him money, of course. The transportation means he was using didn't always provide on-time service.

Will later confessed he was to blame for his problems, a lot of which were based on money.

"I'm partially responsible," he said. "I learned how to be bullish and not bearish. I think I'm pretty good at thinking on my feet. You have to be a risk taker, but you have to learn the limits of what you can take. If you're too risky, you can lose it all. I lost it all.

"Some people are worse. If there are people in the stock market and lose it, the situation can be worse. It's the same thing, it's just more money. It only feels worse because of the amount of money. The shame is overwhelming. It causes them to commit suicide. I have thought about suicide."

When it comes to money, people take things for granted. Some take money for granted. Some spend it at will. Some think once they get one bill paid off and acquire more money life will be grand.

"Yeah, like if they have it, it'll always be there," Will said. "I haven't learned that.

"I don't ever go out and intentionally try to make someone's life miserable or set them on a course for their own financial disasters or financial hardships. My bad financial decisions cause other people financial hardships. I have seen that. It's a shameful thing. It causes those who are close to me financial hardship.

"That's some of the worst shame that a human could have. The worst shame is doing something dishonest like stealing, like I did. I hope I never have to steal again."

Again, you see where this is going. It's all about the money.

"It's fun to have it, and if you don't manage it, which I'm not good at, you're gonna get depressed. I am," Will admitted. "Because I'm always looking to have fun instead of staying balanced. I'm a human being that thinks he can beat the system, but now the system has beaten me. I'm like a bad stock investor. Now my parents know I'm a bad stock investor, which is why they're not investing in me."

Will's parents won a share of a lottery around the time of his ongoing financial struggles. He persisted to say his parents allocated him money to be appropriated for certain expenses, but that they really didn't give him that much. He also persisted to believe he would one day become a millionaire because of their by-chance choice of selecting numbers.

He wasn't reading, *How to Think Like -A- Millionaire* by Mark Fisher and Marc Allen. He simply believed he'd have it handed to him.

All of these experiences caused Will to harbor wavering thoughts on money. He's talked about wanting to acquire large sums of it to enjoy life, but even when family close to him found themselves in that situation, Will felt left in the dark, so to speak.

"He's not getting anything," said his parents' friend who shared their chance luck at selecting numbers all the way to the bank.

In the spring of 2006, when given money by friends designated to pay a man he bought a car from without initially receiving the title, Will promised he wouldn't spend the money on anything else. He agreed to repay the $500 immediately to his friend if the guy he acquired the car from didn't ask him for the money when the title transfer was finally going to be completed. The guy never asked for any more money and gave Will the required documents to secure the title on his own. Nevertheless, Will spent the money he borrowed from his friend anyway. He later searched for excuses why he couldn't pay it back instead of actually being more responsible.

Rod Tidwell, forget your words in the movie *Jerry Maguire*:

"Show me the money."

Those words meant nothing from an integrity standpoint to Will.

"I'm admitting it, I was selfish," Will said at the tail end of 2006. "I spent the money. Hopefully I will never borrow money off someone again when it's all said and done, except for a bank."

And then pay it back, right?

That brings up an interesting concept to ponder:

Promises, promises. "Guarantees" by another person, company or corporation.

Dan Devers, a former University of Arizona pitcher who was drafted by the Minnesota Twins and St. Louis Cardinals, has his own mockery-like expression for unfulfilled promises.

"Check's in the mail. Check's in the mail."

Uh huh. Uh huh.

Do people really have a conscience when they know they did something to put another person in a bind? Especially after telling someone one thing and never following through. What about falling behind in payments? Is it humbling to you? To Will, it apparently was.

"I don't really like money," Will said. "It falls apart when you're not working hard enough."

Laziness and being denied opportunities on countless occasions are two entirely different things. What happens when there are people willing to work hard enough, but aren't given opportunities?

"I explain that as people judging other people," Will said. "All human beings are fit to work."

Unless they're born with a deficiency or disease that physically or mentally prevents them from doing so.

True, people possess at least one talent, gift, passion, craft, skill, trade or desire to lend to society. Society just needs to find a better way of rewarding or making life easier for people who are willing to contribute back to it. And for those people who aren't physically capable of doing so, something suggests there'd be a few good people out there willing to help.

Charity wasn't created by money. It was created by the interlining of a person's heart.

Love.

Contributing to society was the ultimate conquest Paul Kaiser, an individual raised in Hastings, Mich., who became an artist, prioritized as the platform of his life in the late 1980s, early 1990s. That, in a general sense, may seem really vague, but the concept holds plenty of value.

Contributing to society.

Value far more meaningful than money.

Cash confessions

"We are a money-hungry world, that's for sure," said Rev. Andy Gehringer in 2006, while devoting his life as a Catholic priest in Bethlehem, Penn. "I confess greed sometimes."

Gehringer remembers when he was a kid he paid $80 for a pair of Nike hi-top sneakers. Just before the beginning of 2007, he witnessed how kids were spending upwards of $150 a pair. And the terrible part about it is, people will pay that much for a pair of shoes, while some don't have any. Some don't even have any sandals to protect their feet.

Some people walk on streets, out in the outside world with nothing covering their feet. Mother Teresa knows that.

Mother Teresa once said:

"I see God in every human being."

Mother Teresa used to roam the streets of Calcutta, India, doing good deeds for the poor, homeless and destitute. She wanted nothing to do with money, but devoted her life to comforting those who didn't have it. When this compassionate nun, born Agnes Gonxha Bojaxhiu on Aug. 26, 1910 in Skopje, Macedonia, died of heart failure on Sept. 5, 1997 at her bedside in Calcutta a day before Princess Diana's funeral in London, *The Detroit News* and *Free Press* devoted the front page of the next day's paper and three pages inside the main section to Mother Teresa's life. Princess Diana's funeral coverage was masked by a small story at the bottom of page 1 and some inside section coverage.

Mother Teresa had a connection with Princess Diana because she said the royal lady had a soft spot for the poor. Mother Teresa sheltered infants who were abandoned in trash heaps, the story revealed. When the nun was awarded $192,000 as part of her Nobel Peace Prize, she used it to fund her work with the poor. When Pope John Paul II donated a car to her order following a visit to Calcutta, she raffled off the car and used the money to support her ministry.

When it's all over with, all we have to look back on is the memories. The way we devote our lives, our character, our soul, all those things which define us. Mother Teresa humbled herself for the whole world to see, saying things such as:

"When I wash the leper's wounds, I feel I am nursing the Lord himself. Is it not a beautiful experience?"

In 1977, she told reporters, "The poor give us much more than we give them. They're such strong people, living day to day with no food. … We don't have to give them pity or sympathy. We have so much to learn from them."

When accepting the Nobel Peace Prize in Sweden in 1979, Mother Teresa said:

"I choose the poverty of our poor people."

Think about that. Here's someone who actually devoted her life to being around the poor. Could you do it nowadays?

Mother Teresa went on to say:

"But I am grateful to receive in the name of the hungry, the naked, the homeless, of the crippled, of the blind, of the lepers, of all those people who feel unwanted, unloved, uncared for throughout our society, people that have become a burden to society and are shunned by everyone."

Mother Teresa's example of living is what it's all about. It's why after she gracefully departed to higher places, and even while she was here gracing the earth, she received so much attention. A human being doing the "right thing."

Nowadays, there isn't much of that out there.

Chapter 6

Fixing finances

"The spheres in society become corrupted. Family, business, the church, sports ... they become corrupted."
— Dr. Ron Woodworth,
"For Such a Time as This" radio program

Time to revisit inflation. Really, what's the point? Honestly, what does it really solve? Or, maybe more appropriately, what becomes this concept of the ballooning dollar's true effects?

For a lot of people, it's nothing but hardship. One bill overlapping the next. Anxiety, stress and disappointment. Sometimes the worst possible ramifications.

Death.

If under the current economic system there was no such thing as inflation, people wouldn't constantly be struggling just to get by. Constantly struggling to buy.

Inflation is nothing more than an increase in greed. It's a form of worry that, "We need to take care of Number One." Or that idea that, "We need to raise prices to make sure we get ours."

Forget all that economic rhetoric the nation's leading capitalistic figures tell you. Forget this idea that prices must climb to keep pace.

If there were a fixed rate for everything, people wouldn't worry as much. They wouldn't have difficulties biting off more than they can chew. They would be able to keep pace, continue to keep fighting the same fight, and simply survive a little easier.

Without all the worries.

After all, inflation has done nothing but cause problems. In 2008, the America's shrinking dollar provoked talk about more than just a recession. Some considered the times a financial crisis.

A September 2008 report in *The Wall Street Journal* documented the financial windfall that had overcome the United States.

"This has been the worst financial crisis since the Great Depression," said Mark Gertler, a New York University economist who worked with Federal Reserve chairman Ben Bernanke to explain how financial turmoil can effect the economy.

Debt and inflation were two of the biggest issues surrounding the crisis. America's debt was growing out of control. Food costs were on the rise, along with gas and oil prices, yet Congress wouldn't budge on President George W. Bush's 2008 plea to pass a vote for the United States to begin offshore drilling for oil in Alaska. Congressional gridlock, in some ways, was to blame for a poor economy. Offshore drilling during the gas spike's crisis could have saved tons of money.

In 2010, unemployment in the United States was the highest it had been since the early 80s. A perilous sign that not enough money and too much greed was wreaking havoc.

Will Smith's December 2006-released movie, *Pursuit of Happyness*, laid out a pretty good picture of the big picture. His movie depicts what people have been led to believe is the ultimate objectivity in life.

Money.

It was inspired by a true story of how a lack of funds drove a couple raising a young son apart, a man's struggles just to stay afloat and find places to sleep at night constantly being challenged. It was a fight to look after his son's best interest, all the while with society's injustices squeezing tightly on his soul day in and day out.

In the movie, a grizzly-haired Smith, playing the role of Chris Gardner, a San Francisco salesman struggling to survive, made repeated references to Thomas Jefferson's words in the Declaration of Independence:

"The pursuit of happiness"

Smith quizzed himself on this topic, mulled it over scrupulously. After his girlfriend, whom he had a son with, told him over the phone she wanted to leave him, he began to ponder what life was all about.

"I started thinking about Thomas Jefferson and the Declaration of Independence and the part about our right to life, liberty and the pursuit of happiness," Smith said to himself in the movie. "How did he know to put the 'pursuit' part in there? Maybe happiness is only something that we can pursue, and maybe we can actually never have it, no matter what. How did he know that?"

What are people really chasing in life, and how do they obtain happiness?

Smith grew up in the Philadelphia area, where those famous words were laid out and signed July 4, 1776 by 54 men seeking to provide many freedoms, under the blessing and divine guidance of God, for the United States of America. At the time, there were only 13 states, also known as colonies. Pennsylvania was one of them. Philadelphia was the most populated city among those colonies. Philadelphia was our nation's capital at the time.

Smith probably crossed paths with those words thousands of times growing up. His movie, one which he partly directed, hit a home run in its depiction of the realities people constantly are forced to reexamine.

Life, as it has become, is a chase for money in order to survive.

Some people have a whole lot of it. Others have very little or none at all. Yet it has been said we are all created equal.

"… One nation under God, Indivisible, with Liberty and Justice for All."

Think about that.

We're all created equal.

But some people have lots of money. Too much money. Others have none.

If we're all created equal, why should society be based on how much money one has?

Here's an idea:

Start penalizing greedy people. Devise a system that determines how much is enough when it comes to net worth or liquid assets. Once a person reaches that quota, shut off their incoming money supply for a predetermined, extended period of time. Allow others most in need to benefit from the surplus.

It'd be easy to determine a person's liquid assets and personal "toys." Everything could be reported, just as it is today with taxes and other assets. With technology, everyone could have accounts linked to their social security numbers and bank accounts that maintained a running balance of their net worth.

People who don't support this idea are likely people with greedy dispositions and/or have an inability to embrace better solutions. People who simply don't want their money being monitored because they know, deep down, they have more than they need and don't want to forfeit any of it.

They are the same people who many times make themselves "not accessible." People in high places who don't have phone numbers.

Uh huh.

In 2009 and 2010, U.S. President Barack Obama pushed hard for a universal health care plan that would require everyone to have health care. In other words, spill out money to get coverage that turns into an individual case-by-case, hospital-decides-how-it-wants-to-handle-the-situation basis. Employees are individuals. They'll do whatever they want, no matter what "rules" are said to be in place.

Now that's a disparaging concept.

Well President Obama, other world leaders and any incumbents to follow, here's a thought. You want to keep money? You want to make everyone buy a health care plan? Then mandate a law that states anyone who attends college is *guaranteed* a full-time job within three months of graduation. A full-time job in their line of work or area of study.

Here's another idea to build on even further. After you guarantee individuals with the "punched-in-their-educational-timeclock backgrounds," start rationing money out in equal parts to everyone, so long as they are contributing to society, regardless of what they did for a living. In another words, divide the world's total monetary worth and disperse it in equal sums, regardless of career or place in "corporate" or "poverty level" society to everyone. That way, no one is looked at as any better than the next, and all have "equal rights" or "bargaining power," if you will. You could still maintain an educational system, forcing people to attend school through grade 12 and then have a choice whether they wanted to further their education for specialized opportunities. Those who extended their education would obviously be better prepared to assume different responsibilities than others who elected not to. And making college free would obviously postpone starting a career. Those who prepared themselves through college could be given more opportunities than those without a college education.

Allow people to contribute to society with whatever talents or means God blessed them with. People will have different talents and interests because God doesn't fashion everyone the same way. Yes, we're all created equal, but people have different abilities. People have different interests. So stop judging other people in terms of status. Stop judging them in terms of what they do for a living or what man wants to put a value on in terms of what they're worth. If this were truly an equitable society, more people would be given opportunities to share their talents, passions and interests. But with the current problems surrounding economic unrest, cutbacks, money shortages and debt, people aren't always granted the opportunities they're qualified for, let alone deserve.

If under this way of thinking, people are not contributing, they're not entitled to the necessities to live. Or other things in life if you want to call it that. Some argue without money, there would be no way of determining contributions or laziness. That's baloney. Someone could monitor who "punches in their timecard" to contribute to society. And someone might actually enjoy monitoring those people, and then give them a gold star, red star or green star for chipping in. Believe it, there are easy ways to determine if people are contributing to society, with payoffs in more equal amounts. With equal payoffs or equal entitlements, that would create a far more equitable society.

Let's see that would mean …

Farmers can produce crops. So people can eat.

(Heck, people can grow their own food and give it to people that need to eat. And feed themselves.)

A grocer can put out food in the stores. So people can have a place to get their food.

A clothing designer can design clothes. That way people can cover themselves.

A shoe maker can make shoes. That way people wouldn't have to walk barefoot.

A home builder can construct homes. That way people can seek shelter and sleep when they're tired.

Telephone makers can make phones. That way people can talk to each other.

Postal carriers can deliver mail to people when someone wants to communicate with another person by written correspondence.

Pro athletes can put their skills on display for entertainment. Nobody necessarily has to watch. Some can choose to if they're available.

Singers can sing songs. Nobody has to listen. But people can choose to if they so desire.

Teachers can mentor students, teach them about certain subjects or ideals in life they have a passion and educational background specializing in.

A car maker can make cars.

Bus drivers can drive buses.

Pilots can fly planes.

Etc., etc., etc.

That way, everybody has a place in society. People just have to first figure out what that place is and then determine how they're going to lend to society.

It'll start working better when people stop turning their first intentions toward money as the ultimate payoff. When they stop judging others by what they do. Stop putting a value on who's role in society is "more important" than other people.

Here's a start:

Stop judging people.

Stop judging them on what they do for a living. People get judged nowadays for jobs or how much money they make. Or the number attached to their last name. (And yes, social security numbers are attached to credit score numbers.)

Some people are more qualified than others in those positions. People are judged for a multitude of reasons. Sometimes reasons that have nothing to do with qualifications. How many times have you applied for a job and been asked questions about your race or background?

What do those things have anything to do with qualifications?

Those factors become judgments.

There is no such thing as equal opportunity employers. It's about who wants to do what for another person in the current sociological structure.

The shortest chapter in the Bible is Psalms 117. The longest is Psalms 119. They are divided by Psalms 118. There are 594 chapters before Psalms 118 and 594 chapters after it. Add up 594 and 594 and you get 1188. The center verse in the Bible is Psalms 118:8.

Psalms 118:8 reads:

"It is better to take refuge in the Lord than to put one's trust in man."

If this world would stop judging other people, especially as it relates to society and economic standards, and put more emphasis on God, this would be a better place to live.

Or maybe we could just eliminate money altogether.

"Blessed are you who are poor, for the kingdom of God is yours. Blessed are you who are now hungry, for you will be satisfied."

— Jesus
(Luke 6:20-21)

"No one can serve two masters. He will either hate one and love the other, or be devoted to one and despise the other. You cannot serve God and mammon."

Jesus
(Matthew 6:24)

All of the references in this book, be it personal stories, worldwide events, occurences that affect people on a daily basis or the like, hold truths. They are all, in so many ways, related to money. The backlash people have with each other is rooted in money in many cases.

That's why something needs to be done about this unfair society we live in with regards to money. It's simply causing way too many problems.

Maybe you don't agree with this plan. Maybe you don't want to accept the realities people face in society. But if the current money system isn't fixed fast, this world is looking at a whole lot of hurt.

If it is changed, and society contribution-oriented people are allowed to experience life the same way everyone else does, this world will become a lot better place.

NOTE: Anyone who purchases a copy of this book, rest assured, portions of your money will go to charity to help those most in need.

But when world leaders simply just nix the idea of money here on earth and devise an equitable system for all, you can enjoy reading this book for free.